Wildlife
around the
Cuckmere Valley

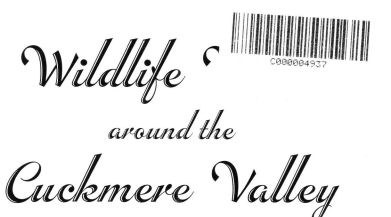

Litlington Church and the Cuckmere River

Patrick Coulcher

S.B. Publications

Wildlife Walks
around the
Cuckmere Valley

To my wife Margaret, who loves the countryside

By the same author:
A Natural History of the Cuckmere Valley The Book Guild 1997
The Mountain of Mist - A novel based on a true story. The Book Guild 1998
The Sun Islands - A Natural History of the Isles of Scilly The Book Guild 1999
Unto the Hills - The History and Wildlife of the South Downs. The Book Guild 2001

First published in 2002 by S.B. Publications
Reprinted 2004, 2008
14 Bishopstone Road, Seaford, East Sussex BN25 2UB
Tel: (01323) 893498

ISBN 1 85770 247 6

Design and Typesetting by EH Graphics (01273) 515527

CONTENTS

Wheatear

Seven Sisters and Hope Gap

Cuckmere Valley in flood near Alfriston, 2000

ACKNOWLEDGMENTS

Many people have accompanied me on the walks in my research for this book. I wish to thank particularly Peter Davys, Dennis Vinall, Jenny Waldron and Dr. Rodney Johnson for their contribution, and also to Andrew Dandridge for the cover picture and for his many sketches. Also included are some of the works of the late Frank Wootton O.B.E. (by kind permission of Mrs Virginia Wootton), Helen Fenton and Sue Davies. Also my thanks to Elizabeth Howe for her painstaking work in deciphering my scribblings and compiling the pages of this book.

All the photographs were taken by myself with the exception of those of the Kingfisher (back page), and the Nuthatch for which I thank Michael Hollings.

P.C.

The Seven Sisters at Birling Gap

INTRODUCTION AND HOW TO USE THIS BOOK

The Cuckmere Valley has always held a fascination for me particularly when, as a young boy, I roamed at will its water meadows and surrounding hills. Its beauty then, as now, confirmed my resolve to do something in my life to protect our countryside. After a busy and rewarding career as a Fighter Pilot in the Royal Air Force, I am now able to devote more time to this objective. My first books on Natural History proved successful and the purpose of this one on Wildlife Walks is to give those who just love walking in the countryside a deeper understanding of Natural History. This book is designed to complement my previous one entitled *"A Natural History of the Cuckmere Valley"* and each walk here corresponds to a chapter of that book.

This work is not for the professional and serious naturalist, although he or she may find something of interest; nor is it designed as a reference book with a detailed description of everything to be found on each walk - to do so would be too repetitious and would result in an encyclopedia. The walker is encouraged to look around him for the wildlife described but inevitably he will miss some species because they are just not there all the time (birds can be particularly elusive), or in the case of many, it may be the wrong season of the year. In describing each walk I hope to give the reader an idea as to the months or season in which some species can be seen. However, a more comprehensive guide as to the best time to see each species is given in the index. Hence in some cases, such as trees, shrubs and non-migratory birds, I have just put Jan - Dec as an indication that they can be seen at any time of the year. In the case of wild flowers, I have shown the best months to see them in flower, and in the case of butterflies the months when they are on the wing.

As far as identification of species is concerned, I have included in the bibliography a number of books which I believe any serious student of nature will wish to have; those particularly useful are asterisked. Binoculars and a book such as *"The Field Guide to the Birds of Britain and Europe"* are essential to learn about and recognise birds. There are many good guide books on wild flowers but I highlighted two which are superb; that by Francis Rose is a small paperback, the second by David Streeter is larger - to be kept in the car or at home. Do buy a good hand lens (10 magnification) to examine the detailed structure of plants, and you will not be disappointed by the sheer beauty revealed in their make-up.

The maps covering each walk are drawn to scale and are designed to highlight most of the places mentioned in the text. For simplicity they are schematic and do not show all the features, roads and tracks. **An additional large-scale map, the O.S. Explorer 123, is essential for the walker, but note that footpaths shown on the maps do not constitute a public right of way.**

Please remember that the countryside belongs to all of us, so do leave it in the same condition as you would wish to find it. Do fasten gates behind you, control dogs, guard against fire, leave no litter, keep to footpaths and protect the plants, trees and wildlife around you.

Finally, I hope this book will help the reader to appreciate the beauty of our countryside and to learn more about the rich diversity of wildlife of this particular area of Sussex, the Cuckmere Valley.

P.C.

AREA MAP OF TEN WALKS

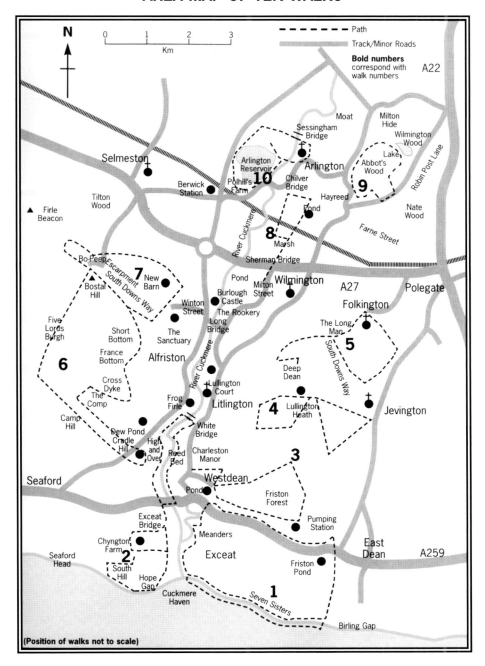

N

| 0 | 1 | 2 | 3 |
Km

- - - Path
Track/Minor Roads

Bold numbers correspond with walk numbers

A22

Selmeston

Tilton Wood

Firle Beacon

Berwick Station

Arlington Reservoir

Polhill's Farm

10

Moat

Sessingham Bridge

Arlington

Milton Hide

Wilmington Wood

Lake

Abbot's Wood

9

Robin Post Lane

Chilver Bridge

Hayreed Pond

Nate Wood

River Cuckmere

8

Marsh

Sherman Bridge

Farne Street

Bo-Peep

Escarpment

South Downs Way

7 New Barn

Bostal Hill

Winton Street

Pond

Burlough Castle

The Rookery

Milton Street

Wilmington

A27

Polegate

Folkington

Five Lords Burgh

Short Bottom

The Sanctuary

Long Bridge

The Long Man

5

France Bottom

6

Alfriston

River Cuckmere

Cross Dyke

Lullington Court

Litlington

Deep Dean

4

Lullington Heath

South Downs Way

Jevington

The Comp

Frog Firle

Camp Hill

Dew Pond

Cradle Hill

High and Over

Reed Bed

White Bridge

Charleston Manor

3

Seaford

Westdean

Pond

Friston Forest

Pumping Station

Exceat Bridge

Meanders

Chyngton Farm

2

South Hill

Hope Gap

Exceat

Friston Pond

East Dean

A259

Seaford Head

Cuckmere Haven

1

Seven Sisters

Birling Gap

(Position of walks not to scale)

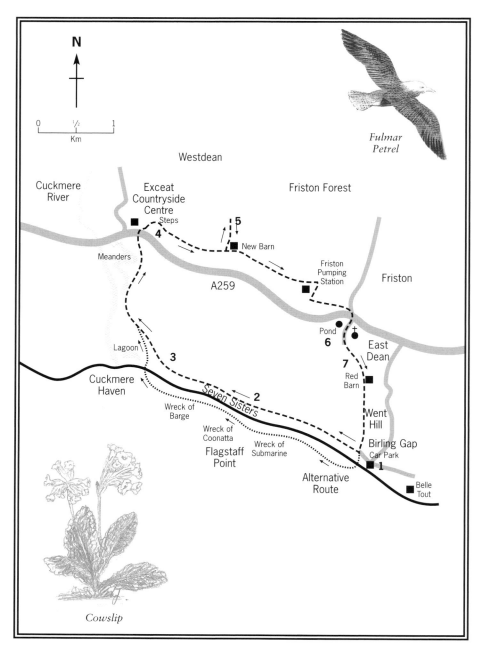

N

0   ½   1
Km

Fulmar
Petrel

Westdean

Cuckmere
River

Exceat
Countryside
Centre

Steps

4

Friston Forest

5

New Barn

Meanders

Friston
Pumping
Station

Friston

A259

Pond

6

East
Dean

Lagoon

3

7

Red
Barn

Cuckmere
Haven

Seven Sisters

2

Wreck of
Barge

Wreck of
Coonatta

Flagstaff
Point

Wreck of
Submarine

Went
Hill

Birling Gap
Car Park

1

Alternative
Route

Belle
Tout

Cowslip

WALK 1   BIRLING GAP, THE SEVEN SISTERS AND EXCEAT

Distance:	13 kilometres.
Route:	Birling Gap, Cuckmere Haven, Exceat, Friston Forest, Friston, Birling Gap. Alternative route for the adventurous is by way of the beach under the cliffs.
Map:	OS Explorer 123: South Downs Way-Newhaven to Eastbourne.
Start / Parking:	Birling Gap Car Park.
Public Transport:	Regular bus service to East Dean, Exceat.
Conditions:	Most of the walk is on firm downland but conditions in Friston Forest can sometimes be muddy. Downland walk on Seven Sisters is up and down over low but sometimes steep hills.
	For the adventurous, an alternative route is to walk along the beach to the Cuckmere Haven to view old wrecks at low tide. This alternative route should only be attempted by those who have experience of walking over large slippery rocks. It is a hazardous route and care should be taken to start as the tide is going out within about two hours of high tide. The tide should be one of over seven metres so that the wrecks are uncovered. It takes three hours to walk the distance under the cliffs. A mobile phone should accompany you!
Refreshments:	Tea Rooms at Exceat Farm and Birling Gap .

THE WALK

As you step out of your car at Birling Gap you will smell the sea and you will sometimes savour the sharper tang of seaweed. Make your way up the unmade road that leads westwards and through the gate and style up to the open downland itself (1).

The grassland here was once lush and long but years of overgrazing has caused many of the birds like the **Skylark** and **Meadow Pipit** to almost vanish. However a fence has been erected in recent years some 10 metres away from the cliff edge to prevent livestock falling onto the shore below. Inside this fence the grass has grown tall and lush and all along the Seven Sisters here you will find the **Field Fleawort** flowering in May. It is easily recognised on account of its rosette of broad oval leaves covered in woolly hairs from the centre of which arises a single woolly stem. This stem, some 10-30 centimetres high, supports a cluster of yellow flower heads branching from one point This uncommon flower has a peculiar propensity to grow near Iron Age settlements whose inhabitants possibly used it for medicinal purposes (the suffix wort signifies this); perhaps also they used it to ward off fleas! Another plant you will see everywhere is the **Viper's Bugloss** with its rough hairy stems and bell shaped blue and purplish-red flowers. It is in bloom from May to as late as October. Extracts from this plant were once used to cure melancholy.

In January and February look out for that marvellous bird the **Fulmar Petrel** as it wheels and dives about these great white cliffs. This bird, the colour of ivory with a light grey back and upper wing surfaces, spends most of the year in the middle of the Atlantic feeding on plankton and small crustaceans; it comes to our coasts in December and January to breed on cliff ledges. Here on the chalk cliffs they nest in small colonies where each pair rear just one chick which after about three months makes it way back out into the vastness of the ocean. Enjoy watching these lovely birds as they hover and dance on the wind that sweeps over these scalloped cliffs of the Seven Sisters.

Much will interest you as you make your way to the first stopping point at the seat beside the memorial stone above Flagstaff Bottom (2). Sit here awhile and admire the scenery all around you. To the east and to the west are the sheer white cliffs of chalk shimmering in the bright light of the sea. Below you is Flagstaff Point, the graveyard of many ancient sailing vessels one of which the *Coonatta* can be seen at low tide on the sand just to the west of the seaweed covered rocks of the Point itself. Around the seat look for the pale pink flowers of the uncommon **Sea Stork's-bill** which is distinguished from other members of the genus by its small, lobed oval leaves. Also growing near the cliff edge are the yellow flowers of the **Wall Rocket**. Both these plants are in flower from May to September.

Make your way westwards along the undulating coastal path that takes you over the remaining four sisters, Brass Point, Rough Brow, Short Brow and Haven Brow. Here, near the top on the westerly slope of the highest Sister at Haven Brow (3) look for the very rare **Wall Germander** plant whose pale to deep purple flowers appear in May and bloom until late September. The plant itself is only about five centimetres high and you are most likely to spot it at the entrance to a rabbit hole where it has shelter from the prevailing winds. Wall Germander was grown in Queen Elizabeth I's reign as an ornate herb for the garden and as such, where it does grow in Britain, it is thought of as a garden escape. Here at its Cuckmere Haven site it is almost certainly indigenous and not introduced by man, for it is a very similar habitat to that on which it grows on the other side of the Channel in France.

The path leads downhill in a north-westerly direction through some mixed scrub of gorse and bramble. At any time of the year you are likely to see the **Stonechat** with its distinctive black head and throat perched on the top of a gorse bush. The male has a distinctive orange-red breast and conspicuous white bar on the wing. The call of the Stonechat is distinctive too, a metallic "chak chak" like two stones being knocked together.

As you descend the slope look down at the meanders of the Cuckmere river for you are likely to see the snow white **Little Egret** with its slow flapping flight across the flat marshes. There **Kingfishers** too are often seen flying low and fast across the meanders seeking small fish in the clear shallow waters. The **Shelduck** is another bird you will see feeding in the fields here, easily distinguished by its green crown and chestnut breast band. In spring it seeks out an old rabbit hole near the cliff edge in which to make its nest.

Follow the white concrete road northwards towards the main A259. About halfway along this road on the right there is a chalk cliff and embankment and above this is a steep downland slope. In late April and early May this is the place to see the **Early Spider Orchid** growing amongst a profusion of **Cowslips**. This actual site is protected by a fence to prevent grazing by livestock. The Early Spider Orchid is one of our rare orchids and is easily recognised because its rich brown flowers with yellow-green and light brown sepals are large in comparison with its overall height of 2-6 centimetres. Near the top of the flower heads are two glistening nectar pouches which look like a pair of eyes.

When you reach the main A259, cross it at the entrance to the car park and make your way to the right past the Exceat Countryside Centre and up to the bicycle hire shop. Beyond this building there is a gate and beyond this is an upward sloping downland pasture over which the path leads you to a gate and an old flint wall with steps to help you over (4).

The view from here is quite breathtaking, especially on an autumn evening when the sun sinks below the distant line of the hills and its orange-red glow reflects off the meanders of the Cuckmere. In the spring the beech trees of the great forest behind you begin to turn green as the pink-purple buds on their sweeping branches unfurl their leaves. Early in the morning when there is little traffic on the main road and a hushed stillness pervades, you may be lucky to hear the wild melodic "tyew-yew-yew" call of a **Redshank**. Once a common breeding bird of the Cuckmere meanders when I was a boy, it no longer nests here because of human disturbance and the predation of crows and foxes.

The path leads down a long flight of wooden steps to the village of Westdean with its small pond. This small Sussex hamlet is steeped in history with its Norman Church and 13th century rectory; its pond was perhaps once the site of a small harbour with a jetty that the troubled Saxon King, Alfred the Great, used as an escape route from his manor house in the village. *At the bottom of the steps follow the gravel road eastwards.*

The Rectory, Westdean

After barely a kilometre down this road you will see two prominent **Scots Pine** trees on the right hand side, their pale red bark distinguishing Britain's only native conifer from many others. Some 20 metres before you reach these pines you will see in the grass on the right of the track the **Vervain** plant, a 30-60 centimetre tall erect and hairy herb with small, pale lilac flowers which appear from July to September. The greyish-white skeleton-like stems of these plants can be seen here throughout the winter. Interestingly, Vervain, although somewhat inconspicuous and nondescript, has enjoyed a magnificent reputation for its medicinal and magical properties; to cure kidney stones, improve eyesight, ward off pestilence and to secure good luck. The Romans in pagan times held Vervain in high esteem; they carried it in processions, offered it in sacrifice and gave it to ambassadors when sent on important missions.

On the left-hand side about 1.2 kilometres along the track you will come across the house and converted barn named New Barn. As a short diversion follow the forest path that leads just east of north up from the west side of the house. This path opens out after about 120 metres and then climbs up to the main east/west forest track (5). On each side are neat rows of 40 to 50 year old beech trees and here under the trees is the place to find the **Yellow Bird's-nest** plant. This strange looking yellow plant with scale-like leaves is devoid of green chlorophyll and lives on decaying organic matter such as beech leaves. The pale yellow or cream-coloured flowers appear at the top of their 5-25 centimetres stem in June and July. The woods here contain one of the largest populations of this plant in Britain.

The wide downland path is full of flowers of many kinds especially in the spring and summer. See how many you can recognise; some like the **Great Mullein, Burdock** and **Hairy Violet** should be easily identified. In February the path is strewn with **Snowdrops** to be followed later by **Bluebells.** This is a delightful place at any time of the year, and particularly in the depths of winter when few people are around, you will feel a great sense of solitude and peace, with the silence of the woodland broken only occasionally by the "zee-zee-zee" of a flock of **Long-tailed Tits** as they seek food amongst the naked branches of the trees.

Retrace your steps back the way you came down to New Barn and continue eastwards along the unpaved road. The woods to your left are of **Beech** and **Douglas**

Long-tailed Tit

Fir, the latter having been first discovered on Vancouver Island (Western Canada) in 1791 and is now considered to be one of the major species in British forests where it is prized for its strong and hard wood, excellent for joinery and construction work of all kinds. In the autumn these woods are a good place to search out fungi of all kinds, **Sulphur Tuft, Puffball, Jew's Ear** and many species of **Bracket Fungi.**

As you approach the Friston Pumping Station the track veers to the north and through an iron gate. About 100 metres further on there is a T-Junction. Turn right and follow the path past two semi-detached cottages, Friston Down and Forest Cottage. **Hart's Tongue Fern** grows all around here, its long strap-shaped bright green shiny leaves bringing colour, character and some beauty to the winter gloom of these dark, dank woods. *Just beyond the cottages there is another T-junction. Turn left here and follow the track as it makes its way steadily uphill until at yet another junction you take the right fork as it traverses steeply up the hill through woods until it emerges on the opposite side of Friston Pond beside the busy A259 (6).* In spring the roadsides here are awash with the yellow of **Lesser Celandine** flowers.

Explore the surrounds of Friston Pond for here you will find numerous species of aquatic plants such as **Water Forget-me-not, Branched Bur-reed,** and the **Great Reedmace** which is some times incorrectly called **Bullrush.** Also found around this pond is the rare **Greater Spearwort** with its stout, hollow stems, and lance-shaped leaves and bright yellow, shiny flowers. *Take the gravelled unmade road that leads south from the pond, past the car-park and over a cattle grid. About 50 metres beyond the cattle grid and gate, break off left from the road and take the path beside a fence that leads south-easterly towards a line of trees. Follow the line of trees southwards and then turn left through a gate that leads to a prominent red-roofed barn named Red Barn (7). Just before this point you will get a good view from the top of the escarpment of the village of East Dean below. The path then leads down past Red Barn towards the stile near the car park where this walk started (1).* There are several ancient trackways and banks of original downland turf near Red Barn and it is worth exploring these to view the numerous species of chalk grassland flowers like **Wild Thyme** and **Birds-foot Trefoil** - see how many others you can identify and also count the number of butterfly species you can find here.

As you pass through the stile and walk down the gravel road back to the car-park see on the right hand side some evergreen shrubs about 2-3 metres high with slender purple green branches and tiny scale-like leaves. This is **Tamarisk,** a native of South West Europe which was introduced to Britain as a shelter hedge plant because of its ability to withstand cutting salt winds. Its pliant stems were once used to make lobster pots and I wonder if these at Birling Gap were originally used for that purpose.

The more adventurous walkers might like to try an alternative, though more hazardous route, for the first four kilometres of this walk.

ALTERNATIVE ROUTE ALONG THE BEACH
UNDER THE SEVEN SISTERS

Start off at the bottom of the steps at Birling Gap at about an hour after high-

tide. Consult tide tables and to get the most out of this alternative route, ensure that the tide is greater than 7 metres. Also it is necessary to have a hard hat (against loose rock falling off the cliff) and a mobile phone for emergencies. *Follow the beach westwards until you come to some old pieces of iron which are the remains of a German submarine.* Captured by the Royal Navy in 1917, it was being towed to the Port of London when its towline broke and was driven onshore. A local man bought the wreck and constructed a railway line along the beach (some of whose sections can still be seen today) to carry the pieces of metal to Birling Gap. *At this point keep under the cliff itself as walking is difficult at lower down the beach.* When the tide is about three-quarters of the way down and just west of Flagstaff Point, a small sandy beach is uncovered and the ribs of a ship can be seen sticking up through the sand. This is the remains of the barque, the *Coonatta* (633 tons) which foundered and broke up in rough weather on 22nd February 1876. It had sailed from Adelaide with a cargo of copper and wool and for a long time its figurehead could be seen beside the pond of Birling Manor until it was sold to an American in 1970. Just over a kilometre further west and lying half-hidden between the shelving rocks can be seen the bottom planks of an old barge. Little is known of its origin but melon sized, square and oblong lumps of granite can be found in its vicinity; these were used as ballast in the ship itself. *The going becomes quite difficult here even under the cliff itself, so be careful.* Under the last great cliff of Haven Brow, note the lines of dark **Flint** which are embedded and evenly spaced up the chalk face as indeed they are all along this coastal stretch. These are the skeletons of minute animals called **Radiolaria** that floated in ancient warm seas some hundred and fifty million years ago. As the earth tilted on its axis (some $2^{1}/_{2}$ degrees every 36,000 years - known as the Milankovitch effect), so the temperature of the sea fluctuated. These Radiolaria flourished only at a certain temperature and as they died, their remains fell to the sea floor so forming layers or bands amongst the more prolific chalk which itself originated from the skeletons of other sea animals, sponges and algae.

Anywhere along this beach you will see a small brown bird hopping around the weed-covered rocks searching for minute scraps of marine life. This is the **Rock Pipit** of which there are about 10 pairs nesting in cliff crevices between Seaford and Eastbourne. *On rounding Haven Brow you will see the wide expanse of shingle (all the remains of flints, shaped and rounded over the millenniums by the waves).* Before rejoining your original walk explore the hinterland of this beach and find many more flowers such as the **Rock Sea Lavender** and **Narrow-leaved Bird's-foot Trefoil**. There are also many commoner species here such as **Scentless Mayweed, Stonecrop, Hound's-tongue** and **Bristly Oxtongue.**

For a moment of quiet contemplation sit on the beach itself and look out at the ever pounding waves as they crash and hiss along the pebble shore.

Wreck of Coonatta

Cuckmere Haven

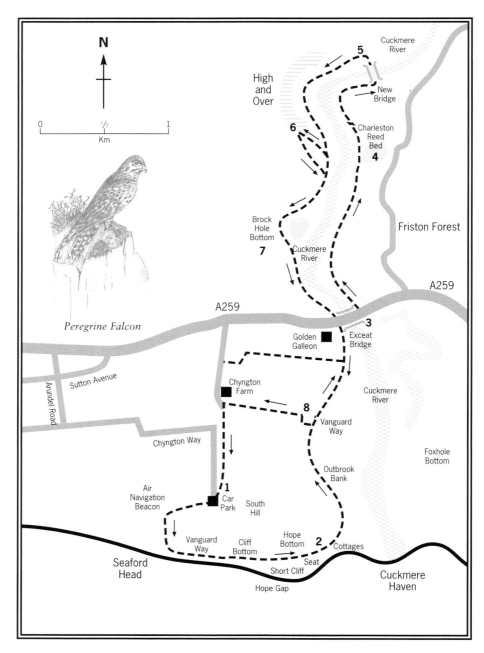

N

0   ¹/₂   1
Km

Peregrine Falcon

Cuckmere River

High and Over

5

New Bridge

6

Charleston Reed Bed

4

Friston Forest

Brock Hole Bottom

7

Cuckmere River

A259

A259

Golden Galleon

Exceat Bridge

3

Cuckmere River

Sutton Avenue

Chyngton Farm

8

Vanguard Way

Cuckmere River

Arundel Road

Chyngton Way

Foxhole Bottom

Air Navigation Beacon

1

Car Park

South Hill

Outbrook Bank

Seaford Head

Vanguard Way

Cliff Bottom

Hope Bottom

2

Cottages

Seat

Short Cliff

Hope Gap

Cuckmere Haven

Distance:	12 kilometres.
Route:	As you enter Seaford from the east on the A259 turn left down Sutton Avenue. Just over 400 metres along Sutton Avenue turn left down Arundel Road until you come to a T-junction. Turn left along Chyngton Way to another T-junction. Turn right up the hill to the car park at South Hill Barn. Walk from this car park to Exceat Bridge via Cliff Bottom, Vanguard Way and Outbrook Bank; then on to New Bridge along eastern bank of Cuckmere River and return to car park via west bank of Cuckmere river and Chyngton Farm.
Map:	OS Explorer 123: South Downs Way - Newhaven to Eastbourne.
Start / Parking:	Car Park at South Hill at TV 504 981, there is no charge for parking.
Public Transport:	None convenient.
Conditions:	Easy walking but muddy along the river banks when wet.
Refreshments:	At Exceat Visitor Centre and the Golden Galleon Public House at Exceat Bridge.

Seven Sisters and Coastguard Cottages

THE WALK

From the car park (1) at South Hill Barn follow the concrete road south westerly towards the Air Navigation Beacon near Seaford Head. Turn left just after the stile and walk along the grassy track towards the sea. Where it joins the coastal path (Vanguard Way), look for a patch of **Pepperwort** with its lance-shaped leaves which clasp the stem and its small four-petalled white flowers which appear from May to August. *Follow the coastal path eastwards, and as you reach the top of a small rise one of the finest views on the South Coast appears before you.*

The full glory of the Seven Sisters are resplendent, their whiteness glistening in the sun, contrasting so strongly with the grey-green of the sea and the bright blue of the sky. This scene subtly changes with the time of day, weather and the seasons and is one that you will never forget.

The downland slopes here are full of flowers in the spring and summer; **Cowslips, Clustered Bellflower, Kidney Vetch, Dwarf Centaury** and **Hairy Violet.** Here in late March and April, large patches of the south facing slopes turn a violet blue as **Ground Ivy** bursts into flower. In May the cliff tops are adorned with tufts of **Thrift,** or **Sea Pink** as it is commonly called. The clumps of rosy-pink flowers blend in so exquisitely with the brown earth and blues and greens of the sky and sea, all with a backdrop of brilliant white cliffs. Halfway down the sloping path to Hope Bottom look for the metre high stout stems of the very poisonous **Henbane** plant. It has an unpleasant smell and hairy, sticky, light green leaves. The drooping yellow and purple flowers bloom from June to August and even in the depths of winter you can see the remains of the plant in the form of tall gaunt-looking greyish-white stalks sticking up through the bare brown soil of the cliff tops.

In April this nature reserve at Hope Gap is a good place to see the influx of migratory birds such as **Wheatears** which are easily recognised with bobbing heads and prominent white rumps as they flit across open ground. The large area of elder, hawthorn and blackthorn scrub are resting places for many incoming warblers such as the **Willow Warbler, Chiffchaff** and **Whitethroat.** *Take a short detour left up the sloping path of Hope Bottom* and listen to the calls of these birds as they delight in catching the plentiful supply of insects after their long flight from Africa. See too if you can find the clumps of the long, lance-shaped, evergreen leaves of the **Stinking Iris.** This plant is common here growing on the banks

Willow Warbler

and under the scrub. The dull purple flowers, tinged with yellow and veined with dark purple, appear in May and June and their orange-scarlet seeds persist throughout the winter. It is also known as the **Roast-beef Plant** because on crushing the leaves it is said to smell of stale beef. **Gladdon** is another name for it, an old English word Gladwyn meaning a sword, referring to the shape of its leaves.

Return to the point above Hope Gap itself and as you walk along the cliff edge path, named Short Cliff, listen out for the high chattering call "kek-kek-kek" of the

Peregrine Falcon which after an absence of some 40 years have recently returned to breed on nearby cliffs. You may catch sight of this wonderful bird of prey with its long pointed wings and slightly tapered tail as it soars and glides so effortlessly in the wide sky. *Sit for a moment on the well-positioned seat beside the path and look at the marvellous views of the Cuckmere Haven and the Seven Sisters (2).*

The route takes you just above the Coastguard Cottages. Follow the Vanguard Way path as it turns northwards and follows the bottom contour of the downland slopes towards the pub at Exceat Bridge, The Golden Galleon; well known for its excellent food and "home brewed" beers. You could follow the path beside the Cuckmere River itself but you will see more butterflies and a greater variety of plants by keeping to the shelter of the hillside. Along this path on a sunny day in April or May you will almost certainly see the male **Orange Tip** butterfly patrolling along the banks and ditches looking for females. The male has the distinctive orange on its wings whereas the female is white with black wingtips. The eggs are laid on plants of the cabbage family such as **Lady's Smock, Bitter-cress** and **Garlic Mustard.** Later on in the year, butterflies like the **Meadow Brown** and **Small Tortoiseshell** may be seen.

In the grass around a patch of Blackthorn scrub just where the steps at Hope Gap go down to the beach, you may find the uncommon **Mountain Stone Parsley** plant with its strikingly pure white flowers arranged in compact heads. It flowers in July and August and its whiteness is such that it glows in minimal moonlight as it attracts night-flying moths of many kinds, hence its common name **Moon Carrot.**

As you walk northwards, to the right of you are extensive salt marshes. In winter these are the haunt of many species of ducks, geese and swans and often you will see a flash of bright blue as a **Kingfisher** dashes just above the shallow ditches looking for small fish. When the weather is very cold these birds migrate from inland to the relative warmth of river estuaries near the sea.

On reaching the Golden Galleon restaurant cross over the A259, turn right over the bridge and then immediately left through a gate and follow the path alongside the eastern bank of the Cuckmere River (3). The river here is tidal and when its muddy banks are exposed at low tide you may see **Redshanks** feeding and other waders such as **Sandpipers, Dunlin** and **Godwits** especially in the winter. To the right of you are large open areas of salt marsh and grassy meadows interspersed with drainage ditches. From late autumn through to early spring these low-lying fields are often flooded and are the haunt of many of our ducks and geese such as **Widgeon, Tufted Duck, Pochard, Mallard, Brent** and **Canada Geese.** Large flock of gulls, including the **Common, Herring** and **Black-headed** gulls, make themselves known as they noisily fly up from the ground when disturbed in their solitude. Flocks of **Lapwings** too, reel about you with their laboured wingbeats, and the occasional **Little Egret** flies low across the marsh. Many of these birds breed further north and beyond the Arctic Circle and come south for comparative warmth and a more certain supply of food. In the summer these wide open spaces are grazed by cattle and then they are largely devoid of birds except for marauding **Rooks** and **Crows.** The **Grey Heron** is to be seen here all the year round standing motionless on orange-yellow legs beside a water filled ditch, ready to stab a small fish with its dagger-like yellow bill. The heron nests in a colony of 30 or more in tall trees nearby.

The path leads you through gates and over stiles until soon a large reed bed appears to your right. This is Charleston Reed Bed (4) and is made up almost entirely of that tall willowy grass **Common Reed Grass** with its razor sharp leaves and feathery flower spikes. Many birds are to be seen here including the **Reed Warbler, Sedge Warbler** and **Reed Bunting.** You may also hear amongst the surrounding scrub the **Willow Warbler, Chiffchaff** and **Nightingale.** All these birds are known to breed in the area of this small Nature Reserve.

Soon New Bridge appears and is a good place to stop and admire the scenery all around you (5). Explore the numerous ditches in spring and you will find plants like **Water Crowfoot** and **Celery-leaved Buttercup** growing on the wet mud or in the water. On the grassy banks in early summer you will also find the **Strawberry Clover** with its distinctive fruiting-heads looking like pink strawberries. High summer here is full of colour with flowers of all kinds alongside the river itself and in the fields and beside the ditches. **Greater** and **Lesser Sea-spurrey** grow in the grass above the mud and **Frogbit, Water Plantain** and **Flowering Rush** can be found in the water filled ditches. The latter is particularly beautiful if you can find it, with its clusters of large rosy-pink flowers and long, slender sword-shaped leaves.

Stand on top of the bridge at high tide in August and September and as your eye gets accustomed to the depth deceptions of colour and reflections in the water, so you will pick out the grey shapes of large **Mullet** feeding on invertebrates in the mud. *Cross over New Bridge and follow the path on the western side of the river in a southerly direction.* In July and August look here for the clumps of **Red Star-thistle** with its distinctive long yellow spines just below the pale purple flowers. This thistle is very rare in Britain and here in the Cuckmere Valley is one of its most prolific sites.

After walking some 60 metres from New Bridge you find yourself looking up at the immensity of the steep slope that forms the wonderful viewpoint of High and Over. The slope is partly wooded but if you have the agility do explore the grassy steep sided slopes for chalk loving plants and butterflies.

Here in early summer you may see the **Green Hairstreak** and later in July you may possible encounter the much rarer **White-letter Hairstreak.**

A slight detour off the main path opposite Charleston Reed Bed takes you up the spur leading to the top of High and Over. Half way up this slope and just above a clump of scrub (6) is the place to look for the uncommon **White Horehound.** This white-felty herb grows in large clumps some 30-60 centimetres high. Its white flowers appear from April to October. This plant was once an important and valued herb and extracts from its leaves were used as a cure for coughs. Amongst the grasses here you will also find **Basil Thyme** and **Calamint.** Sit on the grassy slope and look at the glorious views of the Cuckmere Valley. Between April and September and particularly at dusk, you may hear the rapid "Kikiki" call of a **Hobby** as it swoops effortlessly through the air on narrow swept-back wings looking for its prey of dragonflies or young **Swallows** and **Martins.** This falcon is a migrant from Africa and it has increased in numbers in recent years.

Retrace your steps back to the river side path. All along the bank here and on areas of salt marsh you will find **Sea Aster** with its blue or lilac flowers with yellow centres, **Sea Purslane, Sea Beet, Annual Sea-blite** and **Bucks-horn Plantain;** all are in flower from July to September. *The path becomes narrow just before you reach the artificial pond at Brock Hole Bottom. On the path's western side are open steep chalk banks covered in an array of chalkland flora* and dense patches of **Blackthorn** and **Elder** scrub which give cover for birds such as the **Yellowhammer** and **Chaffinch.** The pond (7) with its small island has a wildlife all of its own - explore its edges and see what you can find. The path soon opens out with a wide, flat area of salty mudflat in front if you. Here in July and August look for that uncommon plant **Sea-heath** with its crinkly five-petalled pink flowers and wiry stems which lie prostrate on the ground.

The path soon diverges away from the river to avoid private property and climbs up the hill to join the A259. Keep to the macadam path to the north of this

Milk Thistle

road and then cross it at Exceat Bridge. Walk through the car park at the Golden Galleon. For the next 800 metres or so follow the original track (Vanguard Way) you came up but at a point opposite Foxhole Bottom on the far side, take the wide track that leads uphill at right angles. This wide track leads to Chyngton Farm and after about 60 metres it turns right and then left. At this sharp bend (8) look in June and July for interesting plants, **Common Mallow** and **Milk Thistle.** The Common Mallow as its name implies is found widely on waste places and beside roads and tracks. Normally it has rose-purple petals, but here there are more extraordinary plants with flowers of a deep violet-blue colour. The Milk Thistle is unmistakable, growing up to 2 metres tall with rosy-purple flower heads surrounded by long spines and with large deep green leaves intricately veined in white. This plant was introduced to the gardens of Britain a long time ago from the Mediterranean and its roots were used as a source of food, together with its leaves and flower heads. It has grown on this site for many years and I hope its presence will be protected and preserved.

As you climb up the path towards the farm on a sunny day in summer, you are likely to see many of the commoner British butterflies. *At Chyngton Farm turn left and follow the road that leads back to the starting point at the car park. As you climb up this long steep road look across to your left at Friston Forest whose colours change so subtly with the seasons and whose secrets form the content of the next walk.*

High and Over and Cuckmere Valley

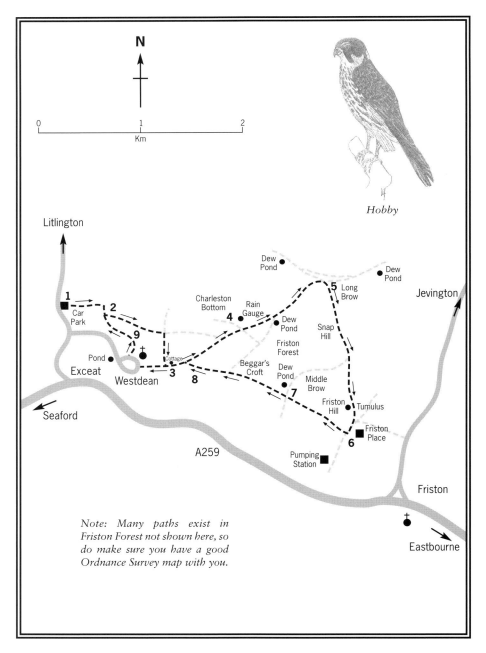

N

0   1   2
Km

Hobby

Litlington

1 Car Park

2

9

Pond

Exceat

Westdean

Cottage

3

8

Charleston Bottom

Rain Gauge

4

Dew Pond

Dew Pond

Friston Forest

Beggar's Croft

Dew Pond

5 Long Brow

Snap Hill

Dew Pond

Jevington

Middle Brow

7

Friston Hill

Tumulus

Friston Place

6

Seaford

A259

Pumping Station

Friston

Eastbourne

Note: Many paths exist in Friston Forest not shown here, so do make sure you have a good Ordnance Survey map with you.

WALK 3 FRISTON FOREST

Distance:	8 kilometres.
Route:	Car park on Exceat to Litlington Road - top of Charleston Bottom - Long Brow - Snap Hill - Friston Place - Beggar's Croft - Westdean - Car park.
Map:	OS Explorer 123: South Downs Way - Newhaven to Eastbourne.
Start / Parking:	Forest Walk car park 800 metres north of Exceat on Litlington Road at TQ 518002. There is a charge for parking.
Public Transport:	None convenient.
Conditions:	Easy walking on undulating flint or grassy tracks.
Refreshments:	Exceat Farmhouse, Seven Sisters Country Park Centre, Golden Galleon Public House, Exceat bridge.

In Friston Forest

THE WALK

From the north-east corner of the car park (1), take the broad track through the trees that leads uphill in an easterly direction. At the junction near the top turn right and then after about 60 metres turn left and follow the fairly straight broad track in an easterly direction. After about 100 metres you come across a wide indentation on the left of the track (2). Stop here awhile and examine the ground and grassy banks and count the many species of wild flowers to be found.

Amongst them you may be lucky to spot the **Adonis** or **Pheasant's-eye** flowering from June to July. This plant has unmistakable scarlet flowers and deeply cut light green leaves.

As you walk along the straight track look on the grassy banks for **Carline Thistle** and **Ploughman's Spikenard.** Both plants flower from July to September, the former recognised by its lance-shaped spiny leaves and yellowish-brown flowers which have an "everlasting" appearance. Indeed the dead flower heads are seen throughout the winter, and if freshly cut when in flower and then dried, they will keep their form and image for years. Ploughman's spikenard, with its tall downy stems (up to one metre high) and clusters of purplish and yellow flowers, has an interesting history. True spikenard was an expensive perfume made from the roots of a Himalayan plant and as such was costly to import; so poor people such as ploughmen who used it for its medicinal properties, found a suitable substitute in a plant that is common on the chalk soils of southern Britain. When its leaves and roots are crushed, it gives out a sweet smelling fragrance; hence its name Ploughman's Spikenard.

About 600 metres from point 2 you will come across a broad path that crosses at right angles. Turn right and follow this southwards down hill for about 300 metres until it dog-legs right to join a main track through the forest that runs west/east.

On your way you will see young **Yew** trees growing on the left hand side and on the grass verges you will find **Dove's-foot Cranesbill** with its rosy-pink flowers, and **Salad Burnet** whose tiny greenish flowers are gathered together in purplish globular heads. The base leaves of this plant, when crushed, smell of cucumber and so it is used as a flavouring in the salad bowl.

The point at which you reach the main west/east Forest path is rich in wildlife (3). **Peacock** butterflies will be seen as they emerge from hibernation on a warm day in early spring, and in the summer months **Painted Lady** and **Comma** butterflies may be seen. Under the **Beech** trees here in late summer you will find the tall spikes of a wild orchid, the **Broad-leaved Helleborine**. The truss of typical Orchid flowers from 10 to 100 in number are held near to the top of the stem and are pink and brown in colour. Quite often in September the flower spike is covered in wasps seeking the rich nectar.

Follow the main track eastwards until you come to a cottage tucked away to your left behind a high hedge. Just beyond the cottage take the left fork (marked "to Jevington" in blue) and follow it gently uphill for about 700 metres.

To your left are rows of beech trees and on your right are many **Wild Cherry** trees and patches of straggling **Clematis** which in winter is easily recognised by the feathery white fruit which forms clusters all over the host plant over which the clematis scrambles. This fruit gives rise to its names, **Old Man's Beard** and **Traveller's Joy,** the latter on account of the fact that in winter the gleaming white fruit stands out amongst bare trees and hedges and thus gives some joy to travellers as they pass by.

The path rises gently uphill in a north-easterly direction and soon you come to a gate beyond which is open downland above Charleston Bottom. On the right just before you reach the gate are masses of the tall **Rosebay Willowherb** with its large elegant clusters of rosy flowers which appear in July and August. It is also known as Fireweed because it so often appears after fire has razed through the woods. In the autumn the seeds of this plant form tufts of long white delicate filaments giving a real sense of beauty to the area. *Pass through the gate to a point beside a rain gauge protected by a small circular barbed wire fence (4).*

Here you are clear of the forest trees that have been so much part of your walk so far, and you are now able to comprehend the wonderful panorama of landscape all around that takes in distant High-and-Over and Lullington Heath. To the north of you, little groups of **Scot's Pine** are highlighted by patches of dark green. Here in summer if the chalk grassland is not too short from overgrazing, you will see many of the downland plants, **Salad Burnet** and **Kidney Vetch** and butterflies such as the **Meadow Brown** and **Common Blue.**

Enjoy the atmosphere here of open space and wide skies before following the path that leads across the plateau of grass to a gate that marks the edge of the Forest. On the other side of the gate the trees and shrubs close in and around you but after a a few hundred metres the path joins a much wider one that emerges from the south-west. The path now widens out with grass verges on either side, a good place to look for wild flowers of all kinds.

Selfheal is one of these and puts out its purple flowers from July to October although I have found it in flower in mid-winter. Self-heal as its name implies was once considered to be one of the most useful medicines for internal and external bleeding. An extract from it was also used as a gargle to cure sore throats and quinsy (tonsillitis).

Just to the south of the junction of the two paths is an old dew pond half hidden by scrub and tall trees.

There are many of these ponds in the forest and some of them are the habitat of a rare amphibian, the **Great Crested Newt.** This is Britain's largest newt and in the breeding season in March and April, the male has a large jagged crest along his back and a striking black spotted orange belly. The best time to see them swimming in the dew ponds is from March to early August as outside this period they are hidden away in the undergrowth and crevices where they hibernate in winter.

The wide path leads you on in almost a straight line to a point where many paths converge just to the west of Long Brow (5).

Here you are deep amidst this great forest and a great sense of isolation prevails. If you turn left here you would soon come across another but much bigger dew pond and if you proceeded even further you would come to the head of Charleston

Bottom which in spring and summer is the breeding ground for many birds such as the **Jay, Greenfinch, Chaffinch** and **Mistle Thrush** to name but a few. In this area you may be likely to catch a glimpse of that fast-flying falcon, the **Hobby.** This bird arrives in mid-April after a long migration flight from central and southern Africa and is soon hawking for insects such as dragonflies in the wetlands of the Cuckmere Valley. Towards the end of May it seeks out an old Carrion Crow's nest at the edge of the forest, usually in a pine tree, which it then occupies to lay its two to four eggs. It's cry of "kew, kew, kew" or a rapid "kikiki" and its scimitar-shaped wings will be its main distinguishing features.

At point 5 take the right hand path that leads in a southerly direction with the tree covered Snap Hill on your right.

As you follow this undulating path note the Holly trees on your left growing among the beech and see the purple flower heads of **Lesser Burdock** which appear from July to September along the edges of the path. In the autumn and winter the Burdock is easily recognised on account of its globe-shaped seed-heads, the familiar "burs" which have hooked bristles which stick onto any rough surface. They become firmly attached to the coats of animals which thus carry them far and wide. The large leaves of Burdock were once used as butter-wrappings and its young shoots, once peeled of their outer skins, can be eaten raw, tasting like new potatoes. The roots can be roasted or stir-fried and can also be used as an ingredient for various drinks including beer; truly a plant with many uses and it is said that the inventor of Velcro fastening got the idea from its seed-heads.

The path leads you up and across some open downland on the spur of Friston Hill where the long grass gives good cover for **Skylarks.** *Turn right at the junction of the road and paths near Friston Place, and when just opposite the large country house itself, turn sharply right and head up hill and through the forest once again (6).*

In the beech woods at the top of the hill look carefully on either side in May and June for the creamy-white flowers of the **Large White Helleborine.** This is another orchid that seems to be reducing in numbers in our southern beech woods. It normally grows some 20 to 40 centimetres tall but here in Friston Forest you will find spikes as high as 60 centimetres. These taller plants are found near the edge of the woods and at the edge of the woodland paths where there is more light. The fresh green oval leaves are easily seen against a brown background of dead beech leaves.

Soon you come across a wide made-up track just beyond Middle Brow which crosses at right angles. Just 100 metres before you reach this crossing look to your left and you will see a fallen pine tree (7).

Notice the holes which have been pecked out by **Woodpeckers,** looking for grubs inside the bark.These holes were probably made by the **Great Spotted Woodpecker** with its black crown and in the male, a crimson nape-patch. This woodpecker has a very loud "kik - kik - kik" call and both sexes drum rapidly on dead branches which resonate. The woodpecker you are more likely to see just about anywhere on your walk through the forest is the **Green Woodpecker**

Green Woodpecker

with its deeply undulating flight pattern and very loud ringing "laughing" voice from which it gets its other name **Yaffle**. It is often seen in open spaces on the ground where it feeds on ants and then as you approach it flies up and into trees, at the same time showing up its magnificent green plumage and brilliant red crown, especially on a sunny day.

After you cross the made-up track (used as a road for forestry vehicles) the path rises steeply.

On you left is an area of **Norway Maple** with its bright spring blossoms and rich autumn foliage. It was planted not only for its timber which is used for making furniture, but also to form an attractive belt of woods beside the forestry road. It has a sweet milky sap much loved by **Grey Squirrels** which do the trees great harm particularly in their crowns. On your right is an area where the trees were "blown out" by the 1987 storm. Now only a few of the original Monterey Cypress trees remain, but most of it has been replanted with deciduous trees and is covered in dense scrub. In spring and summer this is the place to see many of our warblers such as the **Garden Warbler, Blackcap** and **Whitethroat,** and also at any time of the year many of our more common birds such as the **Greenfinch, Linnet** and **Chaffinch.** Butterflies such as the **Red Admiral, Painted Lady** and **Peacock** also are to be seen here feeding on the nectar of thistles, brambles and **Hemp Agrimony.**

The path takes you on to the cottage on your right which you passed on the outward portion of your walk. Some 200 metres before you get to the cottage and just to the right of the path look for the distinctive **London Plane** *tree (8).* This tree has a thin, smooth light green bark which flakes off in irregular plates each summer. Its globular flower heads and large leathery leaves is the only one of its kind in Friston Forest and was planted in 1963 by Peter Davys, the then junior forester.

As you pass the cottage, the harsh penetrating call "kaaa" might catch your attention and looking in the direction of the sound you might see a **Jay** in flight showing off its bold white rump and white patches on its inner wings. As it settles in a nearby bush you may see its distinctive plumage of brownish-pink, black moustache and blue primary feathers. Jays, in the early spring are often seen in small noisy groups and in the autumn they hoard up acorns and other nuts in hideaways like squirrels. These stores of food see them through a harsh winter until the nesting season when their harsh calls send a chill through smaller woodland birds as, like **Magpies,** they do a great deal of harm seeking out and eating their eggs and fledglings.

The path rises gently just beyond the cottage and stops just a few metres beyond the point where earlier in the walk you joined this path. In May, the sides of the path are blue with the flowers of two **Speedwells,** the **Slender Speedwell** and the **Germander Speedwell,** see if you can spot their differences. Look here amongst the tall grass on the bank in June and July for two uncommon vetches, **Yellow Vetch** and **Yellow Vetchling.** Both have solitary pale yellow pea-like flowers but whereas those of the yellow-vetch have no stalk attached the flowers, those of the vetchling are held on long footstalks. The leaves of the former are in the form of pairs of leaflets held on long stems. With the yellow vetchling, the leaves (technically in this plant they are called stipules) are broad and triangular-shaped and almost clasp the main stem.

Follow the path down to the road to the old Norman Church in Westdean, and just beyond the church, turn right and follow the road a short distance until you see a gate in front of you. Pass through the gate and follow the path uphill towards the woodland. At the top turn left along the edge of the wood and follow the sign "to Litlington" (9) (South Downs Way).

About 100 metres along the edge of the wood look just to your right and under a beech tree you will see the shiny green leaves of the **Spurge Laurel** plant. This is a small evergreen shrub typical of chalk-hills and it puts out its smooth yellow-green flowers in January and February. Later these turn into bluish-black berries which are poisonous to man but are eagerly devoured by mice.

The path takes you on through the forest with wide grassy margins in which grow many wild flowers. With these flowers are to be found butterflies such as the **Speckled Wood** and **Orange Tip**. *Soon you find yourself at the point where a wide track leads down to the car park where you started.*

Your walk has taken you through a large proportion of this great forest and I know that you will come away having experienced its sense of loneliness and great beauty. Take this walk at any time of the year and you will feel the changing moods of these woods and even amongst the snow of a still midwinter day the deep, soft silence of tall trees will somehow lift any lingering sense of melancholy. But time to move on to that great nature reserve of Lullington Heath just to the north for our next walk.

Skylark

Jay

In Friston Forest

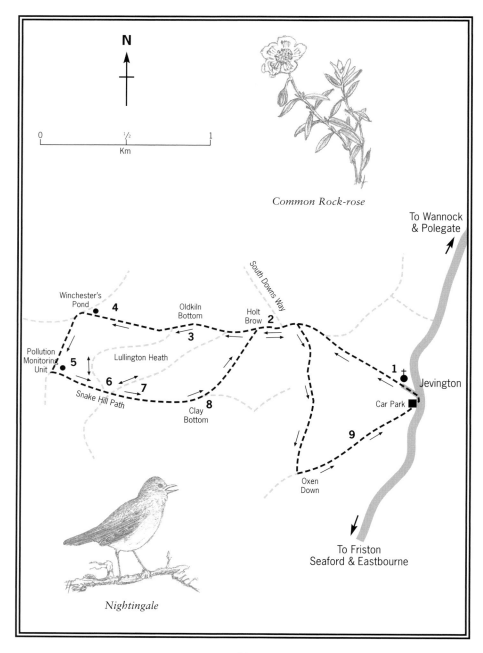

N

0 ____ ½ ____ 1
Km

Common Rock-rose

To Wannock
& Polegate

Winchester's
Pond **4**

Oldkiln
Bottom

Holt
Brow **2**

South Downs Way

3

Pollution
Monitoring
Unit **5**

Lullington Heath

6 **7**

Snake Hill Path

8

Clay
Bottom

1 †
Jevington

Car Park

9

Oxen
Down

To Friston
Seaford & Eastbourne

Nightingale

Distance:	8 kilometres.
Route:	Jevington westwards along South Downs Way to just before Holt Brow then to Oldkiln Bottom - Winchester's Pond then south to Pollution Monitoring Station and then east to Clay Bottom back to Holt Brow and then dog-leg south and north-east back to car park in Jevington.
Map:	OS Explorer 123: South Downs Way - Newhaven to Eastbourne.
Start / Parking:	Park in small car park just to the west of Jevington Road on the southern part of Jevington Village at TQ 562013.
Public Transport:	Very limited.
Conditions:	Undulating downland on excellent paths which can be very muddy after heavy rain or in winter.
Refreshments:	"The Eight Bells", Jevington.

Moschatel

Great Reedmace

THE WALK

From the small car park follow the main road north 120 metres and then turn left up the narrow sunken lane that leads up to the Church (1).

The old flint walls beside the lane are covered with moss and three interesting ferns **Common Polypody, Maidenhair Spleenwort** and **Wall-rue,** descendants of those giant tree ferns that first inhabited dry land over 300 million years ago. The late Saxon Church of St Andrew is surrounded by tall **Lime** trees which were commonly grown in the nineteenth century to bring grace and elegance to country estates. The churchyard itself in spring is splashed with colour from **Snowdrops** and **Daffodils,** and an exotic **Cherry** throws out its blossom of pale pink flowers. Look for a 6 metre high **Weeping Elm** one of Britain's rarest trees, which is probably a hybrid of the **Camperdown Elm** that originated as a seedling at the castle of that name in Angus, Scotland.

Follow the track (The South Downs Way) up past the Church with fields of grazing racehorses on either side. Soon you pass through woodlands of **Horse-chestnut** and **Ash** trees and beside the path in March and April you will see the 10 centimetre tall plants of **Moschatel,** with their yellow-green flowers arranged at the top of the stem, four at right angles to each other like a town hall clock and one on the top facing upwards; **Town Hall Clock** is in fact the countryman's name for Moschatel. *The path curves left and steeply up through tall trees.* At the base of the trees grow massive numbers of that strong smelling, pungent plant known as **Broad-leaved Garlic,** or more commonly, **Ramsons.** Its white flowers appear from April to June.

As the path emerges from the wood near the top of the hill (2) keep straight on and do not follow the main South Downs Way which veers off to the right. At the top of the hill the views are extensive and glorious.

Ahead of you and to the south are the ever-changing colours of Lullington Heath and Friston Forest; beyond, some six kilometres away is the sparkling blue sea of the English Channel. Far off to the west over fields of corn rippling in the wind is Firle Beacon, one of the tallest hills on the South Downs.

Follow the path westwards and down the steep hill to Oldkiln Bottom.

On your left are grassy banks (3) on which grow many chalk-loving wild flowers such as **Common Knapweed, Field Scabious, Wild Thyme, Common Rock-rose** and **Hairy Violet;** all flower in early summer. Earlier, in April and May look here especially for the **Early Purple Orchid** with its 30 centimetres tall spikes of purple flowers and lance-shaped leaves covered in purple spots. In late summer dotted about you here are the red and black berries of the **Wayfaring Tree.**

As this ancient track climbs up from Oldkiln Bottom, look over to your right. In the summer, this area of scrubby grassland, brambles and gorse resounds to the song of **Whitethroats** and **Linnets;** both nest in the area, the former low down amongst the grass and brambles, and the latter higher up in the gorse.

At the top of the hill and tucked away among the scrub on your right is the ancient dew pond called Winchester's Pond (4) which was the traditional water supply for downland sheep flocks.

Now, as part of the Lullington Heath Nature Reserve, Winchester's Pond is a haven for **Dragonflies (The Southern Hawker** and the **Broad-bodied Libellula), Damselflies (The Common Blue), Newts** (including the **Great Crested Newt)** and other aquatic wildlife. Amongst the wild flowers that growth in and around it are the **Branched Bur-reed, Great Reedmace** and the rare **Water Soldier.** This latter plant was once common growing in the middle of the pond; it has leaves resembling those at the top of a pineapple, long and narrow with saw-like edges. Its large white flowers are four centimetres across and bloom from June to August. Visit this place at any time of the year and you will enjoy a sense of freedom and spaciousness and a chance to recharge ones' batteries at the end of a stressful week. I have no doubt myself however, that the best time to visit Winchester's Pond is after a dry spell of weather in July and August; sit here quietly in the grass and watch many species of bird perch on the surrounding shrubs before flying down to the water's edge to assuage their thirst, **Yellowhammers, Whitethroats, Chaffinchs, Mistle Thrushes** and **Willow Warblers** to name but a few. If you are very lucky you may see a **Stoat** creep down through the grass, pause for a moment, and then take its fill of water,

Weasel

its rich brown fur and short black-tipped tail showing up well in the sunlight. Both the Stoat and its smaller relative the **Weasel** are reasonably common on the Nature Reserve but are secretive in habit and seldom seen. They both feed off other small mammals such as mice, voles and young rabbits as well as birds and their eggs.

Where the four paths meet just west of Winchester's Pond there are again glorious views of Firle Beacon and the Cuckmere Valley. Take the grassy path to the left that leads south. On either side of this path are rabbit-grazed patches between the scrub and these are worth exploring for they are the habitat for many chalkland plants including **Wild Thyme, Eyebright, Common Centaury** and **Autumn Gentian,** all flowering in summer and early autumn. Here flitting around the flowers are many butterflies such as the **Small** and **Large Skipper** (June to August), **Small Copper** (April to October), **Common Blue** (June to August), **Meadow Brown** (June to August), and **Marbled White** (July and August).

About 400 metres along the path on the left you will see a set of black railings. Inside is a large concrete cap which covers a deep shaft descending to a huge water supply pipe which takes water to Friston. Beside the cap is a black box which is an air pollution monitoring unit. Surprisingly, its records reveal that this area of Britain is one of the poorest for air quality - the reason remains a mystery. Outside the railings the excavated soil from the shaft and underground shaft has formed a large platform from which you can view most of the Reserve. From this vantage point (5) you will see ponies, sheep and goats (some of which are unusual and rare breeds) which graze the patchwork of grass and scrub.

Just beyond the railings take the track that leads eastwards and downhill.

Look carefully on the edge of the brambles and scrub along this path on a hot, sunny day for our only poisonous snake the **Adder.** This ancient Neolithic trackway is, for good reason called Snake Hill Path. Many of the adders on Lullington Heath have an unusual colour, totally black (Melanistic). This incidence of melanism gives them an advantage over the natural colour (greyish in the male, and more red or brown in the female both with a dark zig-zag line down the back) as black allows them to absorb more solar radiation. They can therefore be more active and feed on days which would be too cool for other individuals. Adders will only bite if trodden upon or picked up and, although very painful, their venom is unlikely to be fatal, but treat them with respect if you encounter them.

To the north of Snake Hill Path look for signposts at (6) and (7) that point to the direction of Lullington Heath itself. Take a detour at either or both of these points and view one of the largest areas of chalk heath remaining in Britain, which in 1955 was established as a National Nature Reserve.

Chalk heath only occurs rarely where acid soils are deposited on alkaline chalk. So here in summer on the heath itself, acid loving plants like **Ling, Bell Heather** and **Tormentil** grow amongst chalk plants which include **Salad Burnet, Weld, Viper's Bugloss** and **Wild Thyme. Tormentil** with its four-petalled yellow flowers has roots containing tannin which is used to treat the "torments" of diarrhoea and sore throats, hence its English name. It was also used once to treat stomach upsets, smallpox, cholera and whooping cough; a truly important plant as a "cure-all" for many ailments. **Weld,** too, with its tall spike of yellowish-green flowers has its uses, as its juice produces a beautiful yellow dye for wool and cotton and it is also the source of the artist's paint called "Dutch Pink". The plants on the heath attract many butterflies, particularly the **Grizzled Skipper** in May and June and the **Grayling** in July and August.

In July and August the Heath is ablaze with the purple of the **Bell Heather** and earlier in April and May the **Gorse** covers areas in yellow and puts out its delicate perfume which smells like coconut. As autumn arrives all the colours change subtly to more mellow browns and greens so you will discover many fungi growing on the Heath such as the tall **Parasol Mushroom** and the small scarlet coloured **Hygrocybe,** or **Scarlet Hood.**

Take care in spring and early summer not to disturb nesting birds which abound amongst the gorse and scrub, but take pleasure watching from a distance **Willow Warblers** as they catch insects and then carry then swiftly but warily to their fledglings in dome-shaped nests near the ground.

Return from your forays on the Heath and make your way back to Snake Hill Path,

Parasol Mushroom

and then on to Clay Bottom (8).

Enclosed by the beech trees of Friston Forest to the south and by tall scrub to the north, this is a good place to come just before sunrise early in May to hear the dawn chorus. As the day begins to lighten, listen to the liquid notes of the **Nightingale** and then as the sky lightens, the air fills with the songs of **Blackcap, Garden Warblers, Lesser Whitethroats** and **Wrens.** If you remain very quiet and still you will see many of these birds as they flit between the bushes.

Take the path that leads up from Clay Bottom through the gate back to Holt Brow and the South Downs Way (2).

As you proceed, there is a large open field on your right and in the south west corner look in the short grass for the diminutive **Frog Orchid** (some 10 centimetres high) that puts out its yellowish-green and brown flowers from June to August. Along the path you may see in May and June the **Green Hairstreak** butterfly. When resting with wings closed, this, our only truly green butterfly, is difficult to see on account of the camouflage afforded by its bright green underwings. The female lays her eggs on a variety of plants which grow nearby, including **Gorse, Common Rock-rose, Dogwood** and **Bird's-foot Trefoil.** Another fast flying butterfly you may see here is the **Dark Green Fritillary** as it settles with wings spread on **Knapweed** and **Thistles** in June and July. The female lays her eggs on the **Hairy Violet** which is common amongst the grass of the chalk downs.

When you reach point 2 of the South Downs Way, take the path that forks off right and about 60 metres further on forks right again. This leads you through the woods and back onto the downs above Jevington.

The views are extensive from Combe Hill to the east and the changing colours of Friston Forest to the west. Enjoy it all, the vista of hills and trees and the wide expanse of sky above; contrasting puffy-white cumulus clouds of summer with the low, dark, leaden stratus clouds of winter.

At a gap in the fence to the left traverse down the side of the downs through cultivated fields of wheat towards Jevington (9), and see how many wild flowers you can count alongside the track.

Some of those very common in cultivated fields 50 years ago can still be found here like the **Field Pansy, Sharp-leaved Fluellen** and **Common Toadflax** all flowering in late summer; but many, such as the **Field Gromwell** and **Chicory,** have now largely disappeared. In high summer the field hedges, where unsprayed by herbicides, are awash with red from a multitude of **Common Poppy** flowers - a truly magnificent sight.

As you reach the car park you contemplate the next walk starting some 7 kilometres away by road, at Folkington, just to the west of Polegate.

WALK 5   FOLKINGTON, WINDOVER HILL, DEEP DEAN, FOLKINGTON

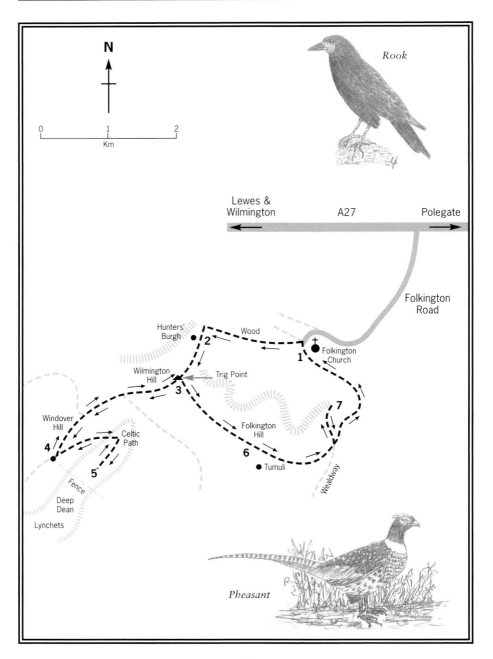

N

0   1   2
Km

Rook

Lewes &
Wilmington   A27   Polegate

Folkington
Road

Hunters'
Burgh   2   Wood

Folkington
Church   1

Wilmington
Hill   Trig Point

3

Windover
Hill

4   Celtic
Path

5

7

Folkington
Hill

6

Tumuli

Wealdway

Fence

Deep
Dean

Lynchets

Pheasant

Distance:	9 kilometres.
Route:	Folkington Church, Wilmington Hill, Windover Hill, Deep Dean, Wilmington Hill, Folkington Hill, Wealdway, Folkington.
Map:	OS Explorer 123: South Downs Way - Newhaven to Eastbourne.
Start / Parking:	Top of Folkington Road next to Folkington Church at TQ 558037.
Public Transport:	Nil.
Conditions:	The first 90 per cent of walk is on firm downland with some steep climbs and descents. The final portion on the Wealdway can be muddy after prolonged rain and in the winter.
Refreshments:	Wishing Well Tea Rooms, Wilmington Giant's Rest Public House, Wilmington.

Lynchets in Deep Dean

THE WALK

As you drive up the narrow lane named on the map as Folkington Road and round the first bend you will see a huge panorama of rolling downland open up before you.

This is one of the most beautiful stretches of chalk grassland on the South Downs. At the end of the lane is the thirteenth century Church of St Peter (1). In March and April the grassy banks here are covered in masses of **Primroses,** their blaze of yellow attracting bees which hum incessantly in the warm spring sunshine.

Just beyond the church and at the end of the lane is Folkington Wood. Take the path just to the south of the wood that leads gently uphill in a westerly direction.

Early May is a good time to walk this path. To your right, under the tall **Beech** trees and beside smaller **Wayfaring Tree,** grow clumps of **Spurge Laurel**, their bright green leaves sparkling in the sunlight. The "blunt, bare-headed, whale-backed Downs", so beloved and described by Kipling, dominate the scene to your left and between the slopes are hollows where a good depth of soil allows tall trees of **Ash** and **Beech** to flourish and form small woods. Across cultivated fields the strident call "kok-kok-kok" of a **Pheasant** breaks the silence of a still day and **Rooks** call out their harsh "kaaa-kau-kau" as they busy themselves in feeding their young. Rooks are thought to be beneficial to cultivated crops because they take out wireworms and other harmful grubs, but at the same time they are very destructive of newly planted corn and are harmful to other bird life, eagerly devouring eggs and nestlings whenever they can find them.

After passing over a stile look on the grassy bank beside the wood.

Here you will find the **Common Rock-rose** and **Early Dog-violet** putting on a display of their bright yellow and pale violet flowers respectively. A **Brimstone** butterfly is quickly spotted, its sulphur-coloured wings and powerful flight pattern making it easy to identify. This butterfly hibernates as such over winter and on the first warm day in late winter it awakes to seek out the nectar of wild flowers.

At the end of the wood you pass over another stile and then walk up an open steep slope of the Downland proper (2).

This is a delightful place to be in June. Wild orchids such as the **Fragrant, Common Spotted** and **Common Twayblade** are to be found growing amongst the downland grasses such as **Quaking Grass** with its purplish triangular shaped spikelets, and **Upright Brome** with its tall stems of drooping flowers shaking in the wind. **Common Blue, Meadow Brown** and **Small Tortoiseshell** butterflies are also seen here in July and August.

Near to the top of the hill you rejoin the ridgeway path which at this point is sunken into the underlying chalk from rain and human traffic over thousands of years. On your right as you climb the hill in a south-westerly direction you will see the oblong-shaped mound called Hunter's Burgh which is the most easterly of the Sussex Long Barrows where Neolithic Man buried his dead.

The grassy banks on either side of the sunken path are covered with wild flowers. Here, in addition to those already seen on your climb up, are **Field**

Scabious, Small Scabious, Round-headed Rampion (commonly known as **Pride of Sussex**), **Carline Thistle** and **Yellow-wort,** all flowering in the summer months.

Soon after passing through a gate you come across the Triangulation Pillar (Trig Point), marking the summit of Wilmington Hill and at 214 metres the highest point in the surrounding area (3).

The views of the distant blue hills of the Weald are magnificent and the wide expanse of sky above combine to give a great sense of freedom and solitude. A **Skylark** can be heard on most days, its musical outpouring of song, so distinctive as the bird ascends in towering flight.

As you traverse this wide ridge above that mysterious carving in the chalk of a man, the Long Man of Wilmington, notice the blue waters of Arlington Reservoir some three kilometres to the north, the subject of the last walk.

Directly above the Long Man and on the highest point of Windover Hill are more burial mounds of ancient man and on the north crest of the hill are the remains of flint mines, constructed some 4000 years ago for the extraction of flints which were used for the manufacture of tools and weapons.

Make your way to the south-west of Windover Hill until you come to a steep deeply-cut path of celtic origin that leads north-east down into the valley of Deep Dean (4). Pause awhile before descending.

Deep Dean; as well as being an important site for wildlife is also interesting historically. Ancient people once lived here and one can see the shape of circular buildings that stood there long before the Romans came. In Saxon times the villagers living in Alfriston, Litlington and Wilmington would have sought shelter in this wooded combe valley whenever raids from the continent or from the Vikings threatened. They would have used this old Celtic path as an escape route to the ridge highway (now the South Downs Way) at the top.

At point (4) explore this plateau of grassland interspersed with scrub.

In August and September you will find the purple flowers of the **Autumn Gentian** or **Felwort.** It grows up to 30 centimetres tall. Later in October you may be lucky to find a much rarer species, the **Field Gentian** with flowers of a more bluish-purple hue. Apart from flowering later in the season and being smaller in height (up to 6 centimetres tall) it can be distinguished by having four petals rather than the usual five of Felwort. Look for it towards the south-west of the plateau where it forms a patch growing on slightly acid soils with **Bell Heather.**

Return to the Celtic path and on your descent into the valley of Deep Dean itself look across to the scrub and trees on the opposite side.

A **Kestrel** hovers above the grassy slope, its wings outstretched and quivering as it seeks out a small vole or mouse. Not far away a **Fox** takes careful, stealthy steps as it proceeds to stalk an unsuspecting **Rabbit.**

As you reach the bottom at the head of the valley, so the isolation and remoteness of this wonderful place becomes apparent.

Kestrel

In the scrub of hawthorn and elder you will see the large

irregular shaped entrances to **Badger** setts, the underground homes of this strong mammal with its short but powerful legs and claws. Interestingly, you will find many **Burdock** plants growing beside the entrances to these setts where the animals have brushed off the clinging burr-covered seed heads from their thick fur.

As you follow the bottom of the valley south-westward look up at the steep bare hillside on your right (5).

Notice the few isolated clumps of the **Wayfaring Tree** which is adorned with red berries in the autumn.

About halfway down the valley your way is blocked by a fence. Beyond it, is strictly private, the land being owned by South-East Water plc.

However, the south-east facing slope above you is of great interest to the naturalist for here you may find three uncommon butterflies, the **Adonis, Grayling** and **Silver-spotted Skipper** as well as other more common species such as the **Red Admiral, Small Tortoiseshell, Small Skipper, Large Skipper** and **Essex Skipper.** All of these butterflies can be seen in July and August when it is sunny except for the Adonis, which if you are fortunate will be seen in late May to June, and from August to September.

On the north facing slopes at the southern end of Deep Dean can be seen the raised banks or terraces which are the result of primitive ploughing by the Celts some 2400 years ago. To get some depth of soil for their crops, they made these terraces known as "Lynchets," derived from a Saxon word meaning "little hill". The flat valley bottom of Deep Dean contains many interesting plants such as the tall **Great Mullein,** its cluster of yellow flowers appearing in June and July. Its seed heads were once dipped in melted animal fat and then used as torches in medieval church festivals. On the slopes of the valley in March and April can be found **Spring Whitlow-grass,** one of our smallest flowering plants, together with another tiny plant the **Early Forget-me-not** which seems to like the slightly acid soil on the soft mossy mounds of the **Yellow Hill Ant.** Later in June and July on these slopes, you will find the beautiful **Bee Orchid** with its greyish-green oblong lance-shaped leaves and flower spike containing two to seven flowers. Each flower bears a remarkable resemblance to a bumble-bee with a broad brown furry lip with deep yellow markings. Around this lip are three pink sepals each with a delicate green line down the middle.

It is time to depart from this remarkable valley with its lovely setting, deep history and abundant wildlife. Climb back up the steep Celtic path.

A **Green Woodpecker** might make its presence known with its loud laughing call as it flies up from a mound of ants to nearby trees on the far side.

Make your way back to the Triangulation Point (3) and just beyond the gate turn right along the broad ridgeway path that takes you atop the broad sweeps of hills so typical of this great Down Country above Folkington. This path provides beautiful views across to the Weald, to Pevensey Levels and to the English Channel beyond Eastbourne.

A light wind and summer cumulus clouds give a serene setting to the **Skylark** which is nearly always heard here. **Meadow Pipits** flit across the open spaces and occasionally the **Corn Bunting** can be seen on a fence post singing its song which sounds like the jangling of a bunch of keys. Interestingly, the Corn Bunting is often polygamous in habitat as the male may have up to seven hen birds as mates. Much of his time is spent on a good vantage point where he can keep watch over his family and defend his territory against rival males.

In the grass beside this wide open trackway can be found the **Harebell** with its attractive blue, bell-shaped flowers. Growing with it and flowering at the same time from July to September, you will find colonies of **Lady's Bedstraw** with its dense clusters of yellow flowers. Earlier in April and May you will find patches of **Crosswort** similar to Ladies Bedstraw, but easily distinguished from it on account of its egg-shaped hairy leaves arranged crosswise in whorls of four up the stem.

About halfway along the track, look for a round barrow, a burial mound just beyond the fence on your right (6).

This mound is now deeply excavated by those seeking artefacts of the Bronze Age people who originally buried chieftains in it. Beyond it are the stark ruins of Hill Barn, an old downland farmstead where there is clear evidence of a walled garden, fruit trees and a place for storing water collected from the roof. A pair of **Chaffinches** have a nest concealed in an old tree growing beside the ancient walls and the cock bird perched nearby gives out a series of anxious chirps "wheet-wheet-wheet".

The path descends in a north-easterly direction.

Look for the **Frog Orchid** in July amongst the grass. In front of you is a large spur of downland, forming quite a large plateau. This was once ploughed up in the 1960s, but has now reverted to open grassland and a few of its original wildflowers have returned. *On your descent, explore the steep hillsides to the north-west of this plateau by following a track which traverses northwards down the hill. You will then discover some of the real gems of this part of the South Downs.*

In June these chalk grassland slopes (7) are the habitat for orchids such as the **Bee, Fragrant, Common Spotted** and **Common Twayblade.** Slightly later in the first week of July the **Burnt Orchid** puts in an appearance. Beside the track and near the top of the hill you will also find a patch of **Spiny Restharrow,** a member of the Pea family, which has erect spiny stems from which grow pink flowers from June to September. The plant has a tough underground root system which used to delay the passage of horse-drawn ploughs or harrows; hence its name.

Having explored this part of the Downs make your way back across the plateau and go over a stile on the eastern edge to join the deep sunken track of the Wealdway, the old smugglers route between Jevington and Folkington.

Adders are quite common along this portion of the Wealdway and can be seen basking in the sun at the edge of the scrub on the western side.

This path is often very muddy after heavy rain but in high summer it gives shade and coolness to the walker.

Beneath its canopy of trees and shrubs you will find the tiny **Moschatel** flowering in March and April and where the path opens out early butterflies like the **Orange Tip, Peacock** and **Small Tortoiseshell** may put in an appearance.

The Wealdway gently curves its way back to Folkington Church where this walk started.

On your left are fields of wheat whose colours change from deep green to a rich gold as the year progresses. Beyond them the whole panorama of near hills are a most wonderful sight. In late summer, sit beside the field edge as the sun sets behind these downs and the sky changes to a deep orange glow. A flock of **Goldfinches,** with their bold markings of red, yellow and black, chatter as they feed on thistle heads. As the hollows of these hills fill with dark shadows, listen to the silence of this scene and let the spirit of this place give you a lasting peace and contentment.

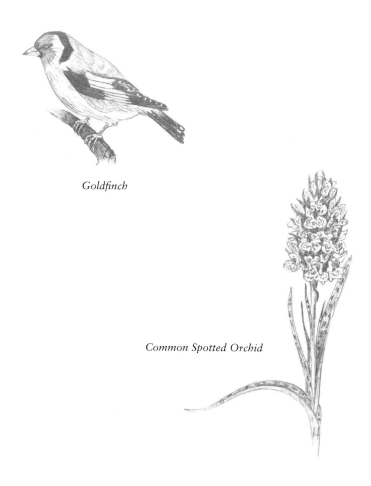

Goldfinch

Common Spotted Orchid

Folkington Church

Bee Orchid

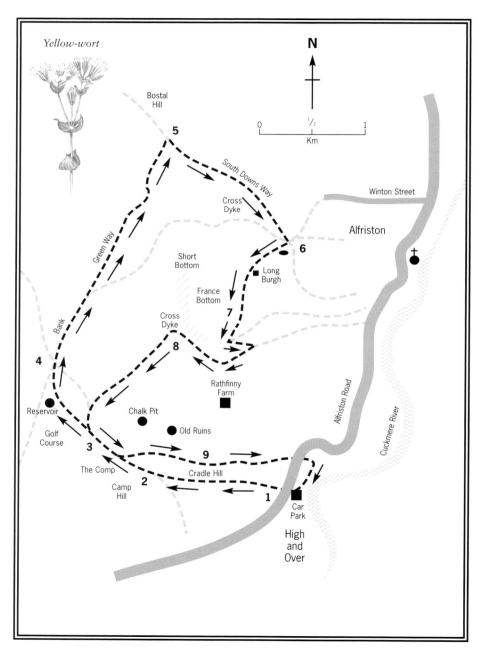

Yellow-wort

N

0   ½   1
Km

Bostal Hill

5

South Downs Way

Cross Dyke

Winton Street

Alfriston

6

Green Way

Short Bottom

Long Burgh

France Bottom

7

Bank

Cross Dyke

8

4

Rathfinny Farm

Reservoir

Chalk Pit

Old Ruins

Golf Course

3

The Comp

9

Cradle Hill

Alfriston Road

Cuckmere River

2

Camp Hill

1

Car Park

High and Over

Distance:	13 kilometres.
Route:	High and Over, Cradle Hill, Camp Hill, Green Way, Long Burgh, France Bottom, Cross Dyke, Camp Hill, The Comp (track), Cradle Hill Bottom, High and Over.
Map:	OS Explorer 123: South Downs Way - Newhaven to Eastbourne.
Start / Parking:	Car park at top of High and Over.
Public Transport:	Regular bus service Alfriston to Seaford.
Conditions:	Firm downland tracks which are undulating in places with some long and short stiff climbs.
Refreshments:	Numerous pubs, tea rooms and restaurants in Alfriston and Seaford.

Cradle Hill

THE WALK

This is a wonderful walk over the South Downs west of Alfriston and in July and August it is particularly noted for the many species of butterflies that you will see.

From the car park at High and Over (1), take the path on the other side of the main Alfriston road that leads westwards along from Cradle Hill. Just before you set off look in the grass edges of the car park for a tall aromatic plant with spikes of small reddish-yellow flowers and deeply cut alternate leaves which have silvery-white silky down on their underneath. This is **Mugwort** which was once in widespread use as a medicinal plant and was stuffed in shoes to prevent travel weariness. Other plants to be found around the car park are **Marjoram, Agrimony** and **Goat's Beard,** all flowering in June and July.

Along the edge of the path above Cradle Hill look for **Perforate St. John's-wort** the commonest of the fifteen or so hypericum species in Britain. It has golden-yellow flowers and the whole plant was once burnt on ritual Midsummer Day fires across Europe as a symbol to "purify" communities and crops. In modern times it is used widely in herbal medicine. A few plants of **Weld,** which is described more fully in chapter 4, can be found beside the path on your right.

Soon after passing through a gate you skirt the southern edge of quite extensive woodland which covers the north facing slope of Cradle Hill.

The soft call of **Woodpigeons** dulls the senses of a hot and sultry summer day, and the harsher calls of a **Pheasant** and a **Green Woodpecker** sound in complete contrast.

Soon you come to a gate (2) near the top of Camp Hill. The path here is called The Comp. At first it is bounded by tall scrub over which **Clematis** grows putting out its glorious seed heads of **Old Man's Beard** which cover the underlying vegetation like snow until winter or even longer. Just five metres past the gate on the left hand side you will see **Large Bindweed** flowering in July and August. It trails up to 3 metres high over this wild hedgerow and has large showy, pure white, funnel-shaped flowers, sometimes with pale pink stripes radiating from their throats. Nearby grows the uncommon **Deadly Nightshade** plant which puts out drooping bell-shaped brownish-purple or green flowers from August to October. Later, black glossy berries appear and these together with the rest of the plant are extremely poisonous. **Upright Hedge-parsley** and **Hogweed** are common here and attract numerous **Hoverflies** particularly in the summer months. The bright rosy-purple flowers of **Wild Basil** catch your eye in many places along the Comp and it is not long before the butterflies begin to be seen in great numbers. You should see in July and August the **Red Admiral, Peacock, Small Tortoiseshell, Painted Lady, Comma, Wall Brown** and **Speckled Wood** butterflies enjoying the sunshine and nectar of the many flowers. *A gap will appear to your right giving you a view across the valley to the north at fields of wheat and barley.* Look carefully in the grass here for **Red Bartsia,** where instead of the flowers being red, they are white. Also found near here are **Scarlet Pimpernel, Perennial Sow-thistle** and **Wild Carrot,** all summer flowering species.

Soon the path opens out (3). On your left is a bank of chalk grassland with a golf course beyond, and below you to the right is an unspoilt steep slope of long grass stretching down to the valley of Cradle Hill below.

This is the place to see chalk downland butterflies such as the **Brown Argus, Chalkhill Blue, Common Blue, Small** and **Large Skippers, Small Copper, Marbled White, Gatekeeper** and **Meadow Brown.** A good time to see all of these is a hot sunny day in late July and August. Occasionally in May, June and late August you may be lucky to see the smallest of Britain's butterflies, the **Small Blue.** So far on our walk we have spotted 17 of the 44 Sussex butterflies but we will visit even better places and see even more species before this walk is completed! Many of the plants that the caterpillars of these butterflies feed on grow here, such as **Kidney Vetch, Horseshoe Vetch, Bird's-foot-trefoil, Dove's-foot Cranesbill, Hairy Violet, False Brome Grass, Tor Grass** and **Cocksfoot.** Many other wild flowers grow here such as the **Field Scabious, Small Scabious, Round-headed Rampion, Eyebright, Common Centaury, Yellow-wort, Felwort** and **Carline Thistle.** Most are in flower from June to August but the last two species are best seen in late summer and the autumn.

Before proceeding along this top path just pause and look ahead at the views to Bostal Hill with fields of wheat and barley turning golden in the sun. To your right are the wooded slopes of Cradle Hill, well named for its shape, and across the Cuckmere Valley are Windover Hill and Deep Dean. Just below you amidst a field of barley is a small chalk pit, its cliffs of white contrasting with the colour of its surroundings, a little oasis of wildlife and a wonderful place as I described in my book *"A Natural History of the Cuckmere Valley"*. Nearby are the stark ruins of farm buildings.

So the walk proceeds along the northern boundary of Blatchington Golf Course and once again the path becomes enclosed with tall scrub on either side. The **Speckled Wood** butterfly is more common here as it prefers shaded areas but there are other butterflies darting here and there looking for nectar, such as the **Gatekeeper** and **Wall Brown.** Beside the track tall patches of **Hemp Agrimony** attract larger butterflies, like the **Peacock** and **Painted Lady,** to their great masses of dull purple flower heads.

Some 600 metres from point 3 an old concrete military road crosses your path and to the left is a square mound indicating an underground reservoir. The path just beyond this reservoir opens out with another path joining from your left. A wooden seat, "In memory of Paul Earl" marks this delightful spot (4).

Sit here awhile and enjoy the views, the butterflies and the wild flowers. Small patches of white are scattered on the path and on close inspection you see they are small mounds of chalk each surrounding a tiny hole which are the burrows of **Field Digger Wasps.**

Nearly opposite the seat another path leads downhill in a north-easterly direction. This is your route and just after passing through a gate, look on your right for the **Vervain** *plant which we also saw on Walk 1. A bank of tall grass with chalk outcrops is on your left.*

This bank is beyond doubt one of the finest stretches for butterflies in July and August as you will see most of those so far mentioned in this walk together with the **Large White, Small White, Green-veined White** and **Dark-green Fritillary.**

Earlier in May you may also see the **Dingy** and **Grizzled Skippers** basking in the sun on patches of chalk with their wings outstretched and even earlier you may see the occasional **Brimstone** and **Orange Tip.** As the path traverses the steep slope the rich plant life of this place becomes apparent. Most of the plants so far described in this walk are here and in addition you will see **Slender St. John's-wort, Burnet Rose, Common Rock-Rose** and **Wild Mignonette.** In June and July the colourful **Six-spot Burnet** moth is quite common here. Burnet moths are extremely poisonous as their bodies contain cyanide. Their striking colour of red and black are a warning to birds not to eat them.

As you descend the slope, cloud shadows sweep across the cultivated fields whose vast areas are only broken up by the downland paths themselves.

The fields here and there have small indentations now filled with hawthorn and blackthorn scrub. These were possible bomb craters from the last war or may have been formed by man when he excavated chalk to spread on acid soils.

At the bottom of the hill the path forks and your route is by the left hand fork (Green Way) which leads you uphill to the South Downs Way at the top of the north escarpment.

There is not much wildlife to see along Green Way but there are wonderful views and the wavering wheat gently rippling in the wind gives you a sense of peace and tranquillity as you stroll gently upwards to the ridgeline.

At the top (5) turn right along the South Downs Way to the ancient crossing of paths at Long Burgh (6). This last kilometre and a half of your walk along the South Downs Way is duplicated in Walk 7. Pause awhile on top of the elongated mound of the long barrow or burial place called Long Burgh.

At this ancient place tall plants of **Mugwort** grow and the **Wayfaring Tree** puts in a colourful appearance in the autumn with its bright red and black berries. On top of the long barrow grows **Wild Basil, Hemp Agrimony** and **Viper's Bugloss.** At the appropriate time of the year many butterflies such as the **Red Admiral, Peacock, Chalkhill Blue** and **Wall Brown** can also be seen here.

At this division of many paths take care to take the main wide track that leads south-westwards and is marked "private road" but is in fact a public footpath that leads past a private house. This broad track at times is bounded either side by high hedges of elder, blackthorn and hawthorn but in places it opens out with views down to the Cuckmere Valley and the village of Alfriston to the west.

As you approach the bungalow on your left you will see the striking flowers of **Japanese Rose,** which in the hedgerow here, has spread from outside the garden to become naturalised. In July and August you will see the large bulbous orange fruits of this spectacular rose.

The track descends down the hillside and just before reaching the house called "France Hill", you cross over the hedge to your right by way of a stile to offer a glorious view of France Bottom below (7). Make your way to the bottom of the hill.

The opposite hillside is covered with scrub mainly of gorse which is a haven for birds such as the **Linnet, Whitethroat** and **Hedge Sparrow.** The short well grazed grass on the hillside here is worth exploring particularly up the valley towards Short Bottom. Yellow flowers of **Smooth Hawk's-beard** and **Lesser Hawkbit** are common from June to September. With luck you will find the **Lesser Centaury** which is less common than the larger species **Common Centaury** and which also grows here. Both have pink flowers which bloom in July and August.

Returning to the path at the bottom of the hill you pass over a stile flanked by **Ash** *trees and traverse the slope eastwards and uphill until you come to a path in front of you near the top of the hill. Cross over the stile and turn right and follow this path westwards.*

The soft purring of a **Turtle Dove** can be heard coming from the woods and thicket to the left. This summer visitor from the continent has declined in numbers over recent years probably due to the reduction of wayside and cornfield flowers from the widespread use of herbicides. The birds rely on the seeds of these flowers as a source of food.

At Cross Dyke (8), not to be confused with a similar place a kilometre or so to the north, the path turns sharply through 90 degrees to the left and descends gently through cultivated fields of wheat and barley to the valley floor. As you descend, look all around you at the magnificent panorama of the South Downs with the sparkling blue sea of the English Channel directly ahead. These fields have few flowers in them but you may find at the edges the **Sharp-leaved Fluellen** with its small yellow and

Turtle Dove

violet flowers and arrow-shaped leaves. This is less common than the similar **Round-leaved Fluellen** which is found also beside the field edges especially below the north escarpment (see Walk 7). Some 200 metres down from the sharp turn, there is a rough piece of land, square in shape, with a thicket and an open space of long grass.

A **Magpie** nests in a hawthorn bush and amongst the grass beside the path you will see bright red patches of **Common Poppy** and also **Black Horehound, Dove's-foot Cranesbill, Field Pansy, White Campion** and **Scarlet Pimpernel.**

At the bottom, the path curves to the right and through a gate. Here is a wasteland with trees, shrubs and long grass in which grows a mass of **Great Willowherb.**

You come to another T-junction and you follow the path to the left which climbs uphill to the south. At first it is enclosed by tall trees with large patches of **Hemp Agrimony** and **Field Scabious** on which **Peacock** and **Red Admiral** butterflies feed. However it soon opens out onto downland with steep grassy banks and small areas of bare chalk. Another wonderful place for butterflies of the kind we have come to expect. You will also see the **Common Lizard** basking in the sun here, and numerous **Common Green Grasshoppers** jump around in the grass

At the top of the hill you rejoin the path called the Comp, near to point 3. Follow

this track south-east for some 200 metres until you see the track that veers off left downhill through a wood. Follow this track down to the valley bottom; most of the way it is enclosed with tall bushes of **Elder, Gorse, Blackthorn** and **Hawthorn. Honeysuckle** and **Clematis** climb over these thickets which in places give way to more open areas where **Ash** and **Sycamore** trees are dominant. Occasionally the sun's rays filter through the foliage and here you will see the **Speckled Wood** and **Ringlet** butterflies.

Small Scabious

At the foot of Cradle Hill, follow the track eastwards until it opens out onto a slope covered in patches of scrub interspersed with large areas of grassland. Sadly this was once only lightly grazed by livestock but at the time of writing and in the two years before, it has been more heavily grazed and many of the butterflies have now declined in numbers. However, you may still see some of the **Skippers** and **Blues** including the rare **Adonis Blue** for there are still good patches of their caterpillars' food plants to be found here. **Rosebay Willowherb** makes a fine showing halfway up the slope and amongst the longer grass near the valley bottom you will see fine patches of **Small Scabious** (some with white flowers), **Lady's Bedstraw** and **Harebell.** The yellow boat-shaped cocoons of the **Six-Spot Burnet** moth can be found here in May attached to grass stems. They hatch out in June and July into vivid black and scarlet moths which we saw earlier in the walk. On the edge of the patches of scrub you may hear the **Chiffchaff** and **Willow Warbler** and if you are patient you will see them together with the **Whitethroat.** Watch them in June as they flit between the bushes seeking insects and grubs to feed their young in well hidden nests.

Follow the path to the busy Alfriston Road where you cross over stiles to the slope overlooking the Cuckmere Valley. Note the yellow flowers of **Tall Melilot** growing beside the road here. *On the other side turn right, keep near to the road and look across to your left at the views of the Cuckmere Valley. You pass by a large tumulus and then enter a wood before you suddenly come out at the car park where you started.*

This walk alone has on a good day shown you over half of the Sussex butterflies (27 in total) together with many downland flowers. Although I have made no mention of orchids on this walk, many can be found in May and June on the grassy slopes and we will get a better look at most of them on the next walk.

Common Lizard

Fulmar Petrels near Birling Gap - February. Page 10

Early Spider Orchid. Page 11   *Germander Speedwell. Page 27*

Meanders of the Cuckmere. Page 11

Red Star-thistle. Page 20

Red Admiral. Page 27

Large White Helleborine. Page 26

Firle Beacon. Page 64

Silver-spotted Skipper. Page 40

Small Skipper. Page 33

Moth Mullein. Page 72

Folkington Downs. Page 32

Speckled Wood. Page 28

Orange Tip. Page 19

Burnt Orchid. Page 41

Cradle Hill in 1992 before overgrazing. Page 50

Chalkhill Blue. Page 47

Musk Thistle. Page 66

Selfheal. Page 25

Comma. Page 24

Nuthatch at nest hole. Page 80

Clouded Yellow. Page 89

Autumn Lady's-tresses. Page 66

Musk Mallow. Page 81

Common Blue. Page 25

Fringed Water-lily on Wilmington Lake in Abbot's Wood. Page 80

Broad-bodied Libellula.
Page 33

Canada Goose. Page 19

Spiked Rampion.
Page 78

Arlington Reservoir and Osprey platform. Page 91

Stinkhorn fungi. Page 82

*Elecampane.
Page 64*

Early Purple Orchid. Page 32

Looking across at the Green Way and Bostal Hill from The Comp. Page 47

The flood below High and Over, 1995

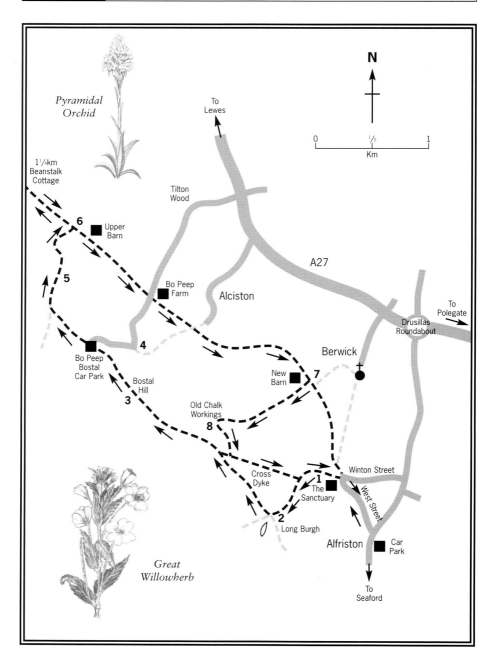

N

Pyramidal Orchid

1¼km Beanstalk Cottage

To Lewes

0   ½   1
Km

Tilton Wood

6 Upper Barn

5

Bo Peep Farm

Alciston

A27

To Polegate

Drusillas Roundabout

Bo Peep Bostal Car Park

4

Bostal Hill

3

Berwick

New Barn **7**

Old Chalk Workings

8

Cross Dyke

Winton Street

1 The Sanctuary

West Street

2 Long Burgh

Alciston

Alfriston   Car Park

Great Willowherb

To Seaford

Distance:	12 kilometres.
Route:	From Alfriston car park walk north up West Street, turn left at The Sanctuary, up to the South Downs Way at Long Burgh. Follow South Downs Way past Bostal Hill. Just after Bo Peep Bostal car park look for the track that takes you down to the path under the north escarpment. Follow this path east-south eastwards to New Barn via BoPeep Farm just beyond New Barn. Take the track back up the escarpment and then down again to the Sanctuary and Alfriston car park.
Map:	OS Explorer 123: South Downs Way - Newhaven to Eastbourne.
Start / Parking:	Car park (small charge) at bottom of West Street, Alfriston.
Public Transport:	Nil.
Conditions:	A stiff climb up to the top of the north escarpment, then level open downland. The track beneath the escarpment is level but can be muddy in places after rain. Near the end of the walk another stiff climb back to the top and then gently downhill to the car park.
Refreshments:	Many tea shops etc. in Alfriston including the White Lodge Hotel and the Star Hotel.

Firle Beacon

THE WALK

From the car park walk up West Street until you reach a house standing on its own called The Sanctuary (1). When the foundations of this home were dug out in 1912 about 120 Saxon graves were uncovered with associated coins, rings, pins and axe heads, swords and knives. This place is the point where five prehistoric paths meet and you follow the wide track that leads west, south and then north up to Cross Dyke and the escarpment of the South Downs. June and July are good months to see the many flowers and butterflies along this way. The pale purple flowers of **Common Mallow** line your route and here they grow in large patches and can be seen from some distance away. Note how the petals of this flower are marked by darker lines radiating to the centre of the flower leading insects easily to the nectar. On either side of the track are cultivated fields of flax, barley and wheat in which few wild flowers can now be found because of the use of modern herbicides. At the field edge where the chemicals have not penetrated you may find the occasional **Common Poppy** and **Field Pansy.**

The path curves southwards and upwards through two deep clefts in the chalk. On the steep banks you will find many species of chalk-loving plants such as the **Carline Thistle, Common Centaury** and **Horseshoe Vetch.** In June you will also see **Common Spotted** and other downland **Orchids.** *You join the South Downs Way near the top at a crossing of six paths (2). This is called Long Burgh because there is a Long Barrow burial mound just to the south. On your climb up to this point there are extensive views of Alfriston and its parish church with the Cuckmere River just beyond. The South Downs Way identified by small blue markers, climbs gently westwards past Cross Dyke and up to Bostal Hill.* To your south, cultivated fields stretch almost to the coast and you look across the area covered by your previous walk. On your right is long grass in which **Meadow Pipits** and **Skylarks** have their nests. Seldom will you fail to hear the skylark's song at any time of the year, except perhaps in deep midwinter.

Along this high path look on the grassy edges for **Lady's Bedstraw, Dove's-foot Cranesbill** and the **Common Restharrow.** The latter is similar to the **Spiny Restharrow** mentioned in walk 5 but lacks the spines and is a much more common species. **Pineappleweed,** a somewhat nondescript plant with greenish-yellow flower heads grows in profusion on the path. This plant came to this country in 1871 from North America and then was spread rapidly everywhere by the growth in modern transport. Pneumatic tyres were soon invented and these picked up the seeds of the plant together with mud and then deposited them both willy-nilly. If crushed between the fingers this plant has a strong smell of pineapple, hence its name.

The views from Bostal Hill (3) are extensive and glorious. To the north the distant dark hills of the Weald beckon you to explore their quiet woods and green fields. To your south, Newhaven harbour and its great breakwater are clearly visible against the deep blue of the sea. Rosy-purple patches of **Rosebay Willowherb** show up against the few patches of grassland where the slopes are too steep to plough. Behind you and ahead are little mounds, the Round Barrows or burial grounds (marked on the map as tumuli) of ancient people. These tumuli are always on the highest point of ground so that they will see the first rays of the sun at dawn, clearly a sign that sun worship was a strong religion at one time.

This is a good point to view the spring migration of birds. So sit on the escarpment slopes on a sunny day in April, preferably with a gentle wind from the south or south-west. Beneath you, flying low and fast from east to west, you will see **Swallows** and **Martins,** in singles and in pairs, following the undulating slopes of these Downs as they make their way inland after their long flight from Central Africa. Swallows begin to arrive in late March a week or so before their close relatives the **House** and **Sand Martins,** and they return slightly earlier too, in September.

Approximately 400 metres to the west of Bostal Hill you come across the car park at the top of the lane that leads steeply down to the main A27 passing Bopeep Farm and Tilton Wood. Take the opportunity to walk down this lane as a short diversion, certainly as far as the sharp bend about 500 metres downhill.

On your right on the way down there is a steep bank on which grow orchids of many species from May to July. About 100 metres down from the top, look in July on this steep bank for the attractive flowers of **Pink** which has grown here since at least 1935 when it was first reported. The Pink is the ancestor of modern Pinks and was probably a garden plant that became naturalised at this spot. *Where the lane bends sharply left pass through the gate on the right (4) and explore the old chalk pit,* another great site for wild orchids especially the **Twayblade, Common Spotted** and **Fragrant.**

Return to the car park at the top and follow the South Downs Way for about 500 metres. Then look for a gate on your right and a track that leads downhill in a northerly direction. Pause awhile before descending and feel the great silence of these hill-tops that have hardly changed since early races of men beyond the skyline of human history lived and left their abundant footmarks. This sunken track, or "bostal" as it is called was such a footmark which was used over centuries as a cattle way, military road, coaching track, and footpath. You will find such bostals in many places on these Downs. *As you descend notice the fenced-off area on your right within which numerous* **Exmoor Ponies** *are grazing (5).* These ponies are a declining species, and were brought in from Devon especially to feed on **Tor Grass** which is a tough, coarse grass that is not eaten by normal grazing livestock. It is conspicuous by its yellowish green colour and with its creeping rootstalk forms patches on open downland and smothers most of the other plants. This attempt to reduce its effect on the ecology of the chalk grassland flora is an experiment which hopefully will succeed.

On either side of the bostal there are good areas of chalk grassland containing many orchids particularly the **Fragrant, Pyramidal** and **Common Spotted.** Other common summer flowering plants here are **Yellow-wort, Salad Burnet** and **Eyebright.** As its name implies, Salad Burnet, although having a somewhat bitter taste, was once used in salads and as a cooling addition to summer drinks. Eyebright, too was an important plant to our ancestors, as a tincture made from its leaves was used as eye drops to clear the eyes of dust and to cure conjunctivitis and other ailments of the eye. If you look at the steep slope of the escarpment you will not fail to see the lines of raised earth that run parallel along the contours. These are caused by a phenomenon known as **Soil Creep** where over hundreds of years the action of rainfall on these hills washes down the soil which then forms into ridges. Often these ridges are made larger by the action of animals and livestock which tend to compact them into convenient paths as an easy way to traverse the slopes.

At the bottom of the hill you pass through a cultivated field just beyond which is an underhill track. If you have the time and energy it is worthwhile walking for about 1¹/₄ kilometres along this track westwards to the Beanstalk Cottage, now a private house, but once a busy public house with stables where the coaches and horses stopped and passengers had a chance to rest overnight. In July beside the remains of the stables you will see the tall plants of **Elecampane** with their striking large yellow flowers and broad leaves covered in soft white velvet underneath. This plant was brought to Britain by the Romans who used its leaves to bind up the legs of lame horses after a hard ride. They also cut up the roots, covered them in honey, and ate them to ward off coughs and colds. It became a common cottage garden in Britain. Interestingly, in recent times the chemical insulin has been found in this species and this is now used in the treatment of asthma.

As you make your way back to point (6) you will look up at the magnificent slopes of Firle Beacon; these "blunt, bow-headed, whale-backed downs" as Kipling so aptly described them. The **Brown Hare** can still been seen occasionally on these slopes.

Brown Hare

The underhill track takes you eastwards past Upper Barn, now a small inhabited house and on to Bopeep Farm. In April patches of **Lady's Smock** can be found along this way. This plant is also known as **Cuckooflower**

because the appearance of its pink, purplish or white flowers herald the arrival of the **Cuckoo** and its distinctive call. The female **Orange Tip** butterfly lays her eggs on the flowers of Lady's Smock so you will see both male (with the conspicuous orange tip to its fore wings) and female (without the orange markings) butterflies on the wing in this area in April and May. The **Comma** will also be seen here as early as February and March if the weather is warm and the sun is shining. Its eggs are laid on nettles or elm. Look out, too, in March and April for the **Brimstone** butterfly as it flies swiftly along the hedgerows looking for spring flowers and their nectar.

You soon come to the crossing of Bo Peep Lane at the farm of that name. This lane joins the A27 at Selmeston and if you have the time follow it northwards for 600 metres to Tilton Wood where many interesting plants are to be found. This is a private wood, but where the lane skirts the eastern boundary, look for the

Lady's Smock   **Greater Butterfly Orchid** along the edge of the ditches on either side. This uncommon orchid has been known in this area for hundreds of years where it frequents damp and ancient woodlands. It puts out its spikes of large white flowers in late May to July. Interestingly these flowers emit a strong sweet smell which intensifies at night to attract night-flying moths. The **Early Purple Orchid** also grows here.

Returning to Bo Peep Farm, follow the track through the farm eastwards. Here after a period of wet weather, it can become very muddy. About 100 metres to the east of the large converted barn at Bo Peep Farm look for the large blue-violet flowers of the **Field Scabious** growing in the hedgerows. This is a much larger, stouter and more hairy version of the **Small Scabious** which itself is found just about everywhere on the chalk. Both are in flower from July to September. Another plant you will find here flowering at the same time is the **Greater Knapweed,** again a large and more striking version of the **Common Knapweed** which is ubiquitous.

The large conglomerate of buildings, known as New Barn soon comes into view. On your left are cultivated fields the edges of which are worth examining for two not-so-common plants, except on chalky soils; the **Round-leaved Fluellen** and **Dwarf Spurge,** both flowering in July and August. These are remnants of a much richer flora in our fields before herbicides were widely used. Look beside the path for an unusual plant and member of the Horsetail family the **Field Horsetail.** The horsetails belong to a primitive and once abundant group of plants which flourished on the planet well before man came on the scene. The stems are hollow and each bears whorls of leafless branches some of which have spores at their tips. These plants appear in the spring and die back in late autumn.

Along this underhill path you will come across many of our common birds such as the **Blackbird, Linnet** and **Robin** but you may also hear and see the **Yellowhammer** which has declined in so many places in the countryside. As you approach New Barn look up at the escarpment of the South Downs and you will see shadows on the slopes marking the indentations of old chalk workings. This is where chalk was excavated to spread on the fields below to break up the thick wealden clays and to make them more fertile, a practice long since abandoned with the introduction of modern fertilisers.

At New Barn (7) you might be lucky to see a **Barn Owl** in wavering flight at dawn or dusk as it seeks its prey of rodents, small birds, frogs or insects. Barn owls have become scarce in recent times but conservation efforts in providing nesting boxes along the Cuckmere Valley have met with some success. Within the old walls of the barn is a wonderful place where in summer **Common Mallow, Tall Melilot** and **Great Willowherb** grow in profusion.

Just 100 metres beyond New Barn on the right is a path which makes its way back up to the escarpment and the old chalk workings which we saw earlier. At first the path is enclosed with high hedges of **Blackthorn, Ash, Sycamore, Crab Apple** and **Elder** but after passing through a gate the path leads on upwards to the open escarpment itself. On your left are large entrances to **Badger** setts which have been excavated out of the chalk banks. These lower downland slopes are heavily grazed but on reaching the mounds and depressions of the old workings, stop awhile for this is a marvellous place for the naturalist (8). Many of our chalk-loving plants grow here such as **Birds-foot Trefoil, Kidney Vetch, Salad Burnet, Eyebright, Carline Thistle, Yellow-wort** and **Squinancywort.** The latter is a small, prostrate herb with four-angled stems bearing narrow leaves in whorls of four. It has tiny funnel-shaped pinkish flowers and gets its name from "quinsy-wort" a herb for sore throats. Many orchids also grow here including the **Bee, Twayblade, Fragrant, Common Spotted,** and in August and September dainty and attractive **Autumn Lady's-tresses** with its white flowers neatly arranged in a spiral around the single stem. With this multitude of different wildflowers it is not surprising that this is also a haven for butterflies and in summer months look out for the **Chalkhill Blue, Common Blue, Gatekeeper, Meadow Brown, Small Heath, Marbled White** and many of the **Skipper** species. Enjoy your short sojourn here and perhaps next time bring a picnic and spend more time in this delightful and special place.

The track follows a deep cleft traversing the steep slope in a south-easterly direction until near the top a wider track leads you back downhill to The Sanctuary and the car park in Alfriston. Along this wider path you will see plants like **Agrimony** with its spikes of five-petalled flowers; this was a plant once used as a herbal medicine for catarrh, digestion problems and snake-bite. Look out beside this track for a tall striking plant with lance-shaped leaves and spines of feathery, greenish-yellow flowers; this is **Weld** which was mentioned before in chapter 4. Also along this way you will see also the large purple drooping heads of **Musk Thistle** which are full of nectar and attract many butterflies and insects. The call "chak-chak" like two stones being knocked together indicates the presence of a **Stonechat** and sure enough there is the male perched on top of a gorse bush. Nearby is the more drab female who at this time in early July is busy attending three of her young who are just beginning to fly. Sometimes on the grassy spaces between the gorse bushes you will see a **Woodcock** probing the ground with its long stout, thick bill looking for worms.

As you descend the track from these hills you can look across to north-east at that great expanse of woodland of which Abbot's Wood forms just a part and which is the subject of your next walk.

Firle Beacon and Bostal Hill

Pyramidal Orchid

Fragrant Orchid

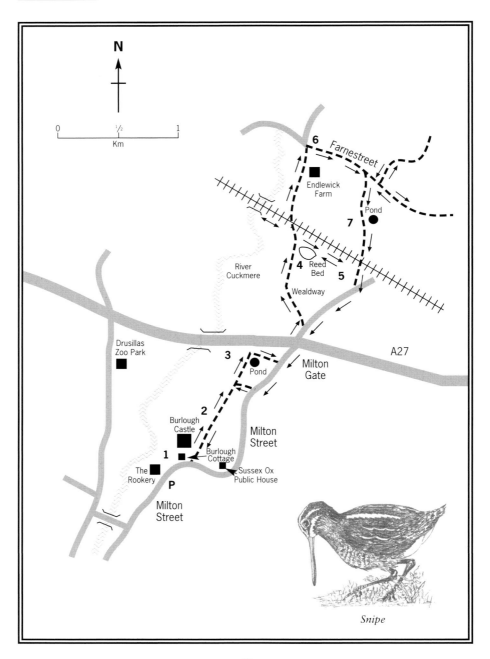

N

0   ½   1
Km

6   Farnestreet

Endlewick
Farm

Pond

7

River
Cuckmere

4   Reed
Bed

5

Wealdway

A27

Drusillas
Zoo Park

3

Pond

Milton
Gate

2

Burlough
Castle

Milton
Street

1

Burlough
Cottage

The
Rookery

Sussex Ox
Public House

P

Milton
Street

Snipe

Distance:	7 kilometres.
Route:	From Lewes along the A27 eastwards to Polegate, turn right at the Drusillas roundabout towards Alfriston. After about 1½ kilometres, turn left and over the Cuckmere River at Long Bridge. Just over the bridge, turn left along Milton Street and after 700 metres, park alongside the road just before it turns sharply right. Walk northwards along the track and just before the A27 turn right and back onto Milton Street. At Milton Gate follow the Wealdway northwards to Farnestreet. Go eastwards along Farnestreet and then after about 400 metres take the path south that leads back to Milton Gate. Cross the A27 and follow Milton Street for 500 metres, and then take the path to your right which rejoins your original path just north of Burlough Castle.
Map:	OS Explorer 123: South Downs Way - Newhaven to Eastbourne.
Start / Parking:	There is no public car park and it is necessary to park on the grass verge at or near TQ 530041. (P)
Public Transport:	None convenient.
Conditions:	Easy walking but muddy in places after rain.
Refreshments:	In nearby Alfriston and Arlington. The Sussex Ox, Milton Street.

Mute swan at nest

THE WALK

Parking on the side of the narrow lane is not easy but with care there is some space available on the verge especially opposite an ancient earth mound and moat called "The Rookery". Having parked safely make your way to the start of the walk just at the point the lane takes a sharp right hand bend, just below Burlough Cottage.

Along the lush road verges of Milton Street grow many wild flowers. In April look out for the tall, stout celery-scented plant called **Alexanders.** It has glossy dark green leaves with solid but furrowed stems, which bear large numbers of small yellow flowers. It was introduced by the Romans from its Mediterranean habitat and was used to add a flavour to Myrrh-like broths and stews and to be eaten raw in salads. Later it was planted in early monastery gardens and became a favoured plant of cottage gardens, its stems were boiled in salted water and made a delicious vegetable when eaten with black pepper and butter.

Just at the sharp corner of the road look for some really tall (20cms) **Cowslips** growing in the long grass. Cowslips were important to our ancestors as their leaves, when young, were eaten in salads and their flower petals were used to make wine which was said to be beneficial for nervous disorders. The roots too, are still used in homeopathy to treat pain and breathing problems and in the past they were used to cure insomnia and to improve memory.

So the reader will appreciate from just these two common roadside flowers, how important Britain's rich diversity of plant life is to our continued well-being. In May the lanesides here, as in most of southern England, are speckled white with sprays of small flowers on downy, tall erect stems. This is **Cow Parsley,** a plant which is used as an herb for garnishing salads, cold potatoes and soups. Be careful not to confuse it with a similar plant **Hemlock** which is extremely poisonous, smells unpleasant and has purple spotted stems.

As you make your way up the deeply cut pathway, note the steeply wooded bank on your left behind the cottage. The area here is the site of a great fortress, Burlough Castle, the origins of which go back into the midst of time. The track on which you are walking was probably the defensive ditch of the castle, protecting it on its more vulnerable eastern side where the ground rises up to Windover Hill. The hedgerow on the eastern side of this track is some 1000 years old, easily established by counting the number of different species of tree and shrub in any 25 metre stretch, each species represents 100 years of age. Here a typical section contains 10 or 11 species made up of **Ash, Buckthorn, Dog Rose, Dogwood, Elm, Field Maple, Hawthorn, Privet, Rowan, Sycamore** and **Wayfaring Tree.**

Along this ancient trackway look for the **Sweet Violet** with its large heart-shaped leaves and sweetly scented purple, blue or white flowers which bloom from February to May. The Sweet Violet reproduces itself not only by forming seeds in the normal course of pollination by insects, but it also throws out long tough runners, several centimetres long, which then take root to form new plants.

The bold majestic bastion of Burlough is omnipresent on your left as the track takes you uphill.

You may well see a **Sparrowhawk** here, perching on the branch of a tree and looking out for a meal of an unsuspecting small bird, mouse or vole. This, one of our commonest raptors, second only to the **Kestrel,** almost became extinct in the 1950's when it declined markedly following the introduction of organochlorine pesticides in agriculture, However, it has made a remarkable recovery with the introduction of controls on the use of pesticides. The Sparrowhawk may be seen on any of these walks since it does breed in and

Sparrowhawk

around the Cuckmere Valley. Winter sightings are common when they are hunting in open habitats, and in early spring females will be active seeking a mate. In ancient times when falconry was a popular sport, many Sparrowhawks were caught and trained to catch **Partridges** and smaller birds. The male Sparrowhawk became known as the "Musket", a term later applied to a firearm.

At the top of the hill there is a ruined stone barn (2). This is a good place to pause for a moment and to admire the views all around.

Across the Cuckmere Valley to the west is the north escarpment of our previous walk and across cultivated fields are the blue waters of Arlington Reservoir and beyond are the wooded hills of the Weald. *At the bottom of the hill past the barn you cross over a stile and a little further on your right is another stile leading into a field which in May is covered in* **Meadow Buttercups** *and in October is full of* **Field Mushrooms.** Near the bottom of this field is a small reed-fringed pond (3). This pond may well have originated when a type of clay called marl was dug out. This clay was used to spread over sandy and acid soils to improve their fertility and texture. The resultant depressions soon filled with water and are now known as **Marl Pits.** This particular pond is surrounded by various species of reed, including the **Great Reedmace,** and by bramble and low scrub. When full, the pond is drained by a small stream which is well hidden by surrounding vegetation. The thick bushes of **Elder** and **Blackthorn** around this pond give good cover for nesting birds such as the **Linnet** and **Whitethroat** and you may be fortunate to see a **Snipe** fly out from the reeds where it has been feeding, probing the mud for worms with its long bill.

Among the many wild flowers growing here you will find **Brooklime, Creeping Cinquefoil** and **Ragged Robin,** all flowering from May to August. Brooklime is particularly interesting with its bright blue flowers and oval fleshy leaves growing in pairs along the stem. The leaves used to be eaten in salads having a similar taste to water-cress, but much stronger. The British Herbal of 1756 suggested that "a large quantity of Brooklime put into beer, while brewing, gives it the virtues of an anti-scorbutic (anti-scurvy) and sweetener of the blood in a very happy manner".

Make your way into Milton Street by way of the stile in the north-east corner of the field and then cross over the busy A27 at Milton Gate. The creamy white flowers of **Common Comfrey** *can be found in May just to your left. Some 60 metres up the unmade road that tracks north-eastwards, you pass through a gate on your left to follow the path (The Wealdway) that tracks north-westwards.* Look in the area beyond the gate and beside the hedge for a rare plant, the **Moth Mullein.** Up to a metre tall this species can be distinguished from other Mulleins by having solitary flowers held at the end of short stems. The flowers appearing in June and July, are normally yellow, but here beside the site of the old Wilmington Airfield they are cream-coloured. Nearby on the right hand side of the track, you will find the pale pink flowers of **Dame's-violet** showing up above the brambles through which it grows. It flowers from May to August. Nearby you will find the metre tall **Aquilegia** with bright blue flowers which appear in May.

The path follows the boundary of the old airfield before descending down into the Cuckmere Valley itself. Again, there are magnificent and immense views, notable for the way in which the colours of the landscape here change with the time of day, weather and seasons. Occasionally you may disturb a **Brown Hare** from its

Lapwing

hiding position as it crouches close to the ground and flees across newly planted wheat. Flocks of **Lapwings** are often seen above these fields in autumn and winter having made their way south from their more prolific breeding grounds in northern England. A **Buzzard** too may be spotted in the spring, soaring and flying in slow wide circles showing off its broad wings and large rounded tail. This bird of prey is extending its range eastwards from its stronghold in Western Britain as the rabbit population (its main diet) increases.

At the bottom of the hill near the river there is a large reed bed on your right made up of the **Common Reed Grass** (4). In the summer months you will hear and see **Reed Warblers** and **Sedge Warblers**. Both species arrive in April and May from Central Africa and make their nests among the reeds. They start their long return journey in August and September. Stop here awhile and listen to their harsh grating chirping calls against a background of the turbulent hissing of reeds in the breeze. Take time to wander through the water meadows to the Cuckmere River itself. See along its banks, **Purple Loosetrife, Marsh Woundwort, Water Pepper** and on the water **Yellow Water-lily,** all flowering in August and September. See also the female **Mute Swan** sitting on her nest amongst the reeds beside the river bank. You will not be able to get close to the nest for the male or "Cob" swan will become aggressive and is likely to attack with menacing and angry hisses.

Make your way up the bank towards the railway track and there you will see a marked crossing point for the path across the lines. Before crossing here take the time to wander eastwards above the reed bed. You will notice that the ground here is sandy in nature. This is the lower greensand of the Weald and on this particular outcrop you will find plants such as the **Subterranean Clover, Parsley Piert** and **Sheep's Sorrel** all in flower in May and June. The caterpillar of the **Small Copper** feeds on this latter plant and the butterfly itself can be seen on the wing here in April and May and again in August and September. Another butterfly to be seen about this sandy wasteland from April to June is the **Grizzled Skipper** whose caterpillar feeds on plants such as the **Wild Strawberry, Silverweed** and **Bramble** all common in the locality.

To the south of the railway line is a stretch of soft marshy ground where natural springs of water filter through the chalk of nearby hills and come to the surface (5). This is a wonderful place in June and July with an abundance of insect, plant and animal life. Look for **Southern Marsh Orchids** and **Common Spotted Orchids,** together with the **Ragged Robin** and **Lesser Spearwort.** A male **Reed Bunting** sings tseek-tseek-tseek-tssisseek from a nearby bush, displaying its black head and throat and white collar. No doubt it has a nest of young hidden in a clump of reeds not far away. The Reed Bunting has declined in numbers in recent years due possibly to a reduction in its preferred habitat of wetlands and attendant rank vegetation. As you retrace your steps back to the point where the Wealdway crosses the railway line, take in the atmosphere of this place; let your thoughts wander into the past and contemplate the origins of the Long Man of Wilmington which looks down at you from its position on the side of the Downs to your south-east. Originally carved into the chalk, he seems to beckon you to come over and take the easy high road over the Downs rather than struggle through the wilderness of forest and scrub that the Weald was at one time.

Make your way back to the railway crossing point. The Wealdway here tracks northwards over several stiles and crosses over a small stream and up past Endlewick Farm to join what was once the old Roman road of Farnestreet. On either side of you on this part of the walk are tall hedges of **Blackthorn, Field Maple, Elder, Hawthorn, Honeysuckle** and others. Patches of **Lady's Smock** and **Red Campion** are seen here in April and June respectively and **House Sparrows** nest in the farm buildings. You will also hear the **Blackbird, Song Thrush, Wren, Robin** and **Hedge Sparrow.** In May this is a good place to hear the **Cuckoo** and you may be lucky to catch sight of one as it flies in a direct manner to perch on a distant bush, somewhat reminiscent of a hawk, with long pointed wings, long tail and small head.

Farnestreet, the ancient route between Pevensey and Lewes Castles, is a wonderful place to explore. As you walk eastwards along the track you are flanked by lush vegetation and hedges of **Hazel, Oak, Elder** *and* **Honeysuckle,** *to name just a few of the many shrubs.* In places tall **Oaks** give shade for **Ferns** of several kinds, **Hart's Tongue** and **Male Fern;** interestingly the word Farnestreet is derived from "The way of ferns". You will not fail to see large holes in the bank here which are the setts or underground homes of the **Badger.** Note also in the more open places the yellow flowers of **Common Fleabane** which in August are favoured by the **Small Copper** butterfly. **Bluebells, Lesser Celandine** and **Primroses** are also common here and a solitary **Pendulous Sedge** plant stands out in the middle of the path where it is damp.

About 500 metres from where you joined Farnestreet you will see a stile and a path which leads south across a large field. This is your route to follow but take time to explore further eastwards along Farnestreet. Some 100 metres further on you come to a track; straight on the path becomes more open but the ancient way turns sharp left and is enclosed with very tall oak trees on either side.

From April to June and later in July and August you may see the **Green-veined White** butterfly flying along the hedge-sides, the female looking for plants of the cabbage (Cruciferae) family on which to lay her eggs. If you explore the more open pathway to the east you will find **Common Hemp-nettle, Greater Stitchwort, Herb Robert, Silverweed** and **Water Mint.** The tall white-flowered **Hemlock Water-dropwort** is common in damp places beside the hedge, as it is along most of the way along Farnestreet.

Retrace your steps and take the path leading off this ancient way across the field. Crossing over a stile the path runs downhill with an old marl pit pond on your left (7). A **Crack Willow** throws its branches haphazardly across the water forming a perfect nesting place for the **Moorhen.** The Crack Willow is easily distinguished from the many other species of willow by lacking the dense covering of silky hairs on its leaves and by the character of its twigs which snap off with a cracking sound. **Water Plantain, Water Forget-me-not** and **Fine-leaved Water Dropwort** can all be found here growing in the water edges and flowering in the summer months.

The path leads you down into a small valley through which a small stream runs. Ahead of you the great figure of the Long Man of Wilmington again dominates the scene from the slopes of Windover Hill. Make your way across the railway line once again and follow the track across the same area of marsh that you explored earlier although then somewhat further to the west. Just south of the railway you cross over a stile and into a field. The path leads you to a tarmacked lane that leads south-west to Milton Gate. In the years just before World War II when this place was the site of the busy airfield of Wilmington, Milton Gate itself was very popular with the public to visit and watch the aircraft take off and land. The sketch on the next page by that great artist, the late Frank Wootton O.B.E., captures the scene at Milton Gate well. As you follow this lane back to Milton Gate look on either side of it amongst the lush vegetation and see how many species of wild flower you can count.

Birds too are plentiful along this quiet road and you should see the **Chaffinch, Yellowhammer, Wren, Robin** and **Whitethroat** to name but a few. *Cross over the A27 road and walk down Milton Street for about 500 metres until you see the house "Windover" on your right. Just past this house is a public footpath sign on your left pointing to the track that leads off westwards from the road. This rejoins your original route just north of Burlough Castle.*

So you return to your car with the satisfaction of having enjoyed a walk with superb views of the South Downs and a chance to find a variety of plants and butterflies.

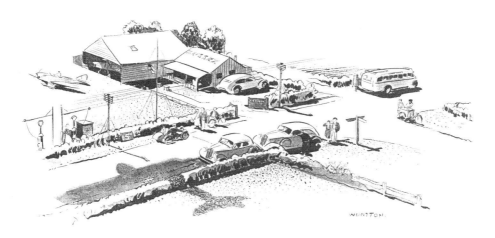

Milton Gate in 1937, showing the main A27 from west to east

Long Man of Wilmington

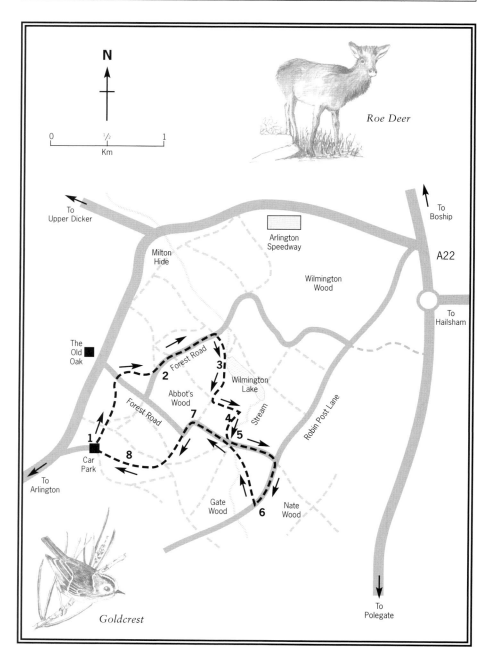

N

0   ½   1
      Km

Roe Deer

To
Upper Dicker

To
Boship

Arlington
Speedway

A22

Milton
Hide

Wilmington
Wood

To
Hailsham

The
Old
Oak

Forest Road

2

3

Wilmington
Lake

Abbot's
Wood

Forest Road

7

4

5

Stream

Robin Post Lane

1

8

Car
Park

To
Arlington

Gate
Wood

6

Nate
Wood

To
Polegate

Goldcrest

Distance:	6 kilometres.
Route:	From the car park follow the yellow footprint path (Abbot's Amble) northwards to the lake. Some 300 metres south-west of the lake at a crossing of paths, walk eastwards away from Abbot's Amble. This path bends to the south after 300 metres. You then come to a major west/east forest 'road'. Turn left along this 'road' until you come to Robin Post Lane. Turn south along this lane for about 400 metres and just before the lane curves to the right take a small path through the wood which tracks northwards to join the forest 'road'. Follow the road westwards for 350 metres. At the T-junction rejoin the Abbot's Amble walk. Follow this south-west and then westwards back to the car park. Make sure you have a good map of the area because it is easy to become disorientated with the many paths and trackways!
Map:	OS Explorer 123: South Downs Way - Newhaven to Eastbourne. Also Forestry Commission guide map available at car park.
Start / Parking:	Park in car park provided by the Forestry Commission just south of the Old Oak public house in Arlington. (Small charge).
Public Transport:	Nil.
Conditions:	Flat, with well marked tracks which can be muddy in places especially in the winter and early spring.
Refreshments:	Old Oak Public House in Arlington.

THE WALK

At the car park (1) pick up one of the Guide Maps entitled Abbot's Wood and follow the route northwards by way of the yellow footprints called Abbot's Amble. You soon enter the woodland proper and just about 100 metres after crossing over a public bridleway look on your left for an oak tree 20 metres tall.

Look for the lines of holes around its trunk, between 1-5 metres high, where a bird, probably a **Great Spotted Woodpecker,** has taken sap from the trunk. Just beyond, on the right of the path, you will see a small fenced off portion of the wood in which the rare **Spiked Rampion** plant grows and flowers in May or June. Spiked Rampion which you will see again near the lake is a native of central and southern Europe and was probably brought to nearby Michelham Priory by visiting monks who knew of its culinary properties. From the Priory it spread to nearby woods and lakesides, its only foothold in Britain being in East Sussex.

Just before the path curves sharply to the right to cross over another main track, look to your left to see the **Yellow Pimpernel** with its five-petalled solitary flowers on long stalks which appear in May and June. Earlier in April in this general area of the wood you will see **Wood Anemones** and **Bluebells.**

Your path now twists and turns as it makes its way north-eastwards to Wilmington Wood and Wilmington Lake.

In May and June you will hear and probably see the **Goldcrest,** a fairly common breeding bird in the wood. Its small basket-like nest is suspended hammock-style about 3 metres off the ground from the branches of a coniferous tree. The Goldcrest has a distinctive high-pitched call "zi - zi - zi" and outside the breeding season it is often seen roaming around the trees with **Blue, Great** and **Long-tailed Tits.** In places the path opens out, and where the sun forms dappled patches on the ground, look out for the **Speckled Wood** butterfly which is on the wing any time between April and September. *Just before the path joins the main forest road (2),* there is a large open space with young **Silver Birch, Ash** and **Broom.** Here in late June and July when the sun is shining you will see many butterflies such as the **Red Admiral, Ringlet, Meadow Brown** and **Silver-washed Fritillary.** This latter butterfly is a real gem with its large orange-red spotted wings showing up strongly as it flies fast across your path and amongst the sunlit spaces of the oak trees.

The path now joins the Forest Road, a vehicular access for the Forestry Commission which manages this large ancient woodland. On the right hand (east) side in the ditch under the shelter of tall trees look out for the **Lesser Spearwort** with its yellow flowers in June. Later in July and August the **Common Fleabane** and **Gipsywort** come into flower here. In August the golden yellow ray-florets of the former attract the **Small Copper** butterfly. Interestingly, Gipsywort got its name from the fact that the juice of the plant was

Lesser Spearwort

used as a black dye which was applied by gypsies to darken their skin. In the damper places along the road you will see tall spikes of **Common Spotted Orchids,** some almost white, but most a pale pink. In July you will find the hairy and strong-smelling **Hedge Woundwort** with its spikes of reddish-purple flowers. A **Jay** gives a harsh cry as it flies in a laboured manner across your route; this bird is very common in the woodlands and you are sure to see it again. A woodpecker is heard "drumming" on dead wood deep amongst the trees; you may see it flying in an undulating pattern and noting its red undertail you recognise it as the **Great Spotted Woodpecker.**

On your left on the ground amongst the tall conifers is a mound of pine needles which is "heaving" with the largest of our species of ant, the **Wood Ant.** The worker ants are busy building up their mound and taking food to the numerous Queens contained in the complex labyrinth of intercommunicating chambers beneath ground level. Throughout the coniferous parts of the wood you will find these ants nests, some over a metre high. You will come across the ants in many places across your path forming their own trackways as they forage far and wide from their nests.

Along the wider sunlit paths just about anywhere from May to August, look out for the 16 millimetre long larvae of the **Glow-worm.** The female hides under leaves and debris during the day, but at night, she crawls onto vegetation, puts out a yellow-green light to attract the male which has wings and can fly. The larvae of the glow-worm feeds on slugs and snails by injecting them with a digestive juice which enables it to suck up all the fluid remains. Glow-worms in the middle of the last century were so common in the countryside that in some places people could read by their light. Now they are quite rare, probably because of the loss of our meadows and grassland.

When you have come to a crossing of paths, follow the sign to Wilmington Lake. As you turn right to the south-east look out for that tall hairy plant, **Great Willowherb,** also known as **Codlins-and-cream** because its rosy petals were the colour of codlins (cooking apples) with a trace of creamy whiteness underneath. Along this stretch you will also see again **Gipsywort, Yellow Iris** and **Lesser Spearwort.** In July and August your eye will be attracted to the small rounded heads of a deep purplish-blue flower, the **Devil's-bit Scabious.** The roots of this plant were once boiled in wine and used to treat snake-bite and the plague. The roots are short and come to an abrupt end and monks used to say that "the root was once longer until the devil bit away the rest from spite, envying its usefulness to mankind".

Soon the noise of trickling water is heard filtering through the foliage of this peaceful place. The source of the noise is soon apparent as the large expanse of water forming Wilmington Lake comes into view (3). The lake, after rain, overflows down a concrete sluice and into a smaller stream. The **Osier Willow,** with its pale yellow-green stems, grows nearby and from the lake itself comes a harsh honking sound of a pair of **Canada Geese** which make their nest on the small island in the middle. A pair of **Mallard Duck** take off with the splashing of webbed feet on the surface and a **Moorhen** calls out "kttok" as it makes for cover in the surrounding reeds. It seems the birds resent the intrusion of their space in their idyll of water surrounded by dense trees where the sense of timelessness is only disturbed by the changing seasons. In July the surface of the lake is the colour of golden yellow from the flowers of the **Fringed Water-lily.**

The lake is one of three ponds believed to have been built in the thirteenth century for the purpose of raising fish to supply Battle Abbey and nearby Michelham Priory. It fell into disrepair in the sixteenth century after the dissolution of Battle Abbey and was neglected until 1964 when it was restored by the Forestry Commission. If you walk beside its southern edge you will come across the remains of a medieval "stew" pond, in the form of a small area of water, aside of the main lake, in which fish caught from the larger lake were placed to be kept alive until they were needed for cooking.

You will find many aquatic plants growing along the edge of the lake including the uncommon **Greater Spearwort** and **Skullcap,** both flowering from July to September.

Your path takes you in a southerly direction past the lake. On your left is a large open space where **Douglas Fir** and other conifers have been felled for timber. The purple flowers of **Selfheal** are evident alongside the path and in the open area **Rose-bay Willowherb** puts in a colourful appearance of rosy-pink flowers.

About 100 metres beyond the lake just to the right of the path, a **Nuthatch** has taken over an old woodpecker's nesting hole some 12 metres up in a tall **Oak**. With binoculars you can see where the original nest hole has been made smaller by the new occupant with the use of mud, thus ensuring that unwanted intruders are kept out. Just beyond this oak, behind the bank on the right, is another small patch of the **Spiked Rampion.**

Just beyond the open patch, leave the Abbot's Amble path and turn left where there is a sign "No Riding". Follow this path easterly for 250 metres when it turns sharply right to a southerly direction.

At this point (4) you will see some ancient **Hornbeam** trees with large distorted and twisted trunks caused by years of coppicing. The very hard white wood of this tree was formerly used for ox-yokes, cogs, mallets and wooden screws and it still serves as butchers' chopping blocks.

Soon your path comes to a crossing of the main forest road and you turn left to follow the road eastwards (5). Here it is worth resting a moment as you are deep amongst this great forest, once known as Lindhersse and part of the vast Saxon forest of Andredesweald which stretched across the south of England from Kent to Hampshire. Now the forest is made up of woods, Wilmington Wood, Gate Wood, Nate Wood and of course Abbot's Wood. The peace here is profound, the only noise being the whisper of rustling leaves and the call of birds. A few metres along the road on your right you will see the distinctive large hairy-toothed palmately-lobed leaves of the **Lady's-mantle** which puts out clusters of small yellow-green flowers from June to September. Nearby grow tall pale pink spikes of **Common Spotted Orchids.**

You may hear the purring "roor-rr" of a **Turtle Dove** which was once a common summer visitor but has been on the decline for many years. However, you are certain to hear the repeated "coo-coo-coo" of the **Collared Dove** in these woodlands and see its pale buffy colour and black line on the sides of the neck, quite different from the more colourful Turtle Dove with its grey-brown head and back and turtle-shell appearance of its wings. As you walk along the road peer through the bushes on your left and you will see a vast expanse of scrub amongst which young trees have been planted. On an early summer evening you may just be lucky to hear the loud and distinctive "churring" of a **Nightjar** for this uncommon bird does make its nest on the ground in the area.

The forest road bends to the right and soon you see a gate beyond which, crossing at right angles, is the ancient track Robin Post Lane. Turn right and follow the lane south-westwards through a leafy canopy of **Hornbeam** *and* **Sweet Chestnut** *trees. After about 300 metres just as the lane curves to the right look for a small path leading northwards through the wood (6).* Follow this path through **Hornbeam** and **Hazel** coppice, the floor of which is covered in **Bluebells** in the spring. Soon a winding stream, cutting deeply into the ground, appears on your left. In this area you may see the nesting boxes of **Dormice,** put up by the Forestry Commission to encourage these rare little mammals to breed. They spend most of their life in the tree canopy coming down only to breed and to hibernate in the winter. Dormice do not like disturbance so do not be tempted to interfere with their nesting boxes. The path here can be very muddy in winter and you may well see the hoof prints of the **Roe Deer** embedded in the mud. Each hoof leaves two toe marks some 4 centimetres long which converge and narrow at the front. The path soon joins the forest road at point 5. Turn left here and follow the road north-westwards.

On your left in July and August look out for the attractive pink flowers and deeply cut leaves of **Musk Mallow.** In damp places alongside the path the **Lesser Spearwort** grows in abundance. Also growing here beneath the shade of tall trees, and just about everywhere else on your walk, you will not fail to spot the long slender stems and pale pink, almost white, flowers of **Enchanter's Nightshade.** The small flowers are remarkable in that all their parts are in twos; two lobes, two petals, two stamens and two seeds. You may well see that handsome butterfly the **White Admiral** here in June and July swooping low over vegetation to take nectar from bramble flowers and then soaring upwards to perch high up in the trees. The female lays her eggs singly on **Honeysuckle** on which the caterpillar feeds; you may see these butterflies just about anywhere in the woods where patches of sunlight reach the ground.

The path soon joins the original Abbot's Amble walk at a T-junction (7) where you turn left to follow it in a semi-circle back to the car park.

To your left are tall conifers including **Western Hemlock** and **Scots Pine** and along the edge of the walk are more **Common Spotted Orchids** and **Lesser Spearwort.** To your right is deciduous woodland made up mainly of **Oak.** Patches of **Water Mint** can be found in damp places here and just about anywhere beside the woodland tracks.

As the path curves to your right just after crossing the public bridleway, so the surroundings become more open with **Silver Birch** and **Grey Willow** predominating (8). Although you are likely to see and hear many of our warblers in many other similar places on your walk, this is a particularly good locality to pause awhile and listen. A **Chiffchaff** put out its distinctive "chiff-chaff-chiff-chaff". The beautiful songs of the **Nightingale, Blackcap, Whitethroat** and **Garden Warbler** can also be heard here, and in late spring and early summer they are busy constructing their nests in the abundant vegetation all around. If you look closely in moist shady places here and in other areas in July and August you will find the **Lesser Skullcap** plant with small purplish-pink flowers, a different species to the **Skullcap** seen earlier. Another more common plant found just about anywhere on the banks and path edges is **Lousewort** with a trailing stem and hairless, much divided feathery leaves. It has pink or reddish flowers which bloom continuously from April to August.

Throughout your walk you will see many species of **Fern**, the most frequent of which are the **Common Polypody** which grows on old boundary banks, and **Male Fern** and **Broad-buckler Fern** which grow in places where the woods are damp and dark. As autumn draws near, and the rains come, so the woodland floor takes on the smell of damp decay, a mustiness that suggests mould and the death of a place that was once full of life and vitality. However, this is just a passing phase of nature for as the leaves decay so **Fungi** of many varieties begin to form on old wood and decaying vegetation. So look out for such species as **Sulphur Tuft, Stinkhorn** and **Oyster Mushroom.** Look particularly on the wood of live trees to see if you can find the larger bracket fungi such as **Dryad's Saddle** and **Many-zoned Polypore.** A good guide to identify ferns and fungi can be found in the bibliography.

So we have walked through this vast expanse of trees and scrub; perhaps even on a still frosty morning in winter or on a sultry hot afternoon in summer you will see some of its abundant wildlife and feel its magic quality and deep sense of history. Of course you will see much, much more than is possible to describe in this short chapter and as you become more familiar with the area and your confidence grows, so you will be tempted to explore beyond just Abbot's Wood to such delightful places as Nate Wood and Wilmington Wood. I have deliberately not tried to describe the great history of this place; to do so would require another book, of interest perhaps to the historian, but not to the casual walker. However, it is worth remembering that for a thousand years or more this whole area was once harvested for its **Birch, Hazel, Hornbeam, Beech** and **Oak** which were the source of firewood and timber for nearby homesteads, villages and towns. **Osier Willows** were grown to provide material for making baskets to carry pottery fired near Robin Post Lane. More recently thousands of soldiers camped in Abbot's Wood for the D-Day invasion of Normandy and huts and strongpoints were constructed together with an emergency landing strip for small aircraft.

The stillness and peace can be felt anywhere and one can easily imagine how the poachers of centuries past, like the Cacklebury Gang, could work silently on moonlit nights with dogs and nets, each man knowing his part and each dog trained to perfection.

Time to move on to the last chapter and walk the more open spaces around Arlington Reservoir.

Wilmington Lake

In Abbot's Wood

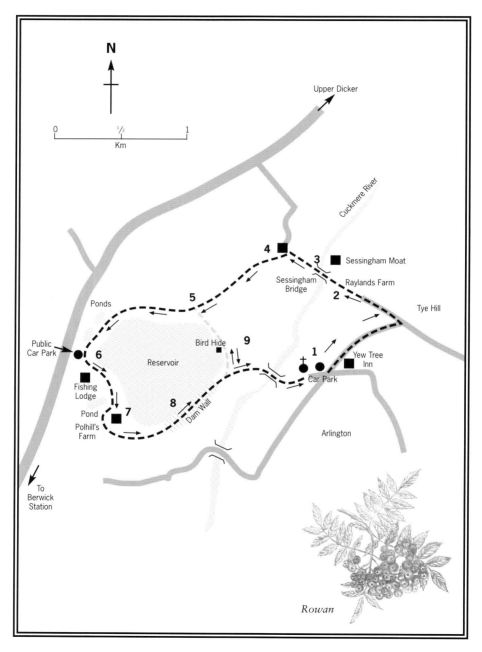

N

0   ½   1
Km

Upper Dicker

Cuckmere River

4

3   Sessingham Moat

Sessingham Bridge

Raylands Farm

2

Tye Hill

Ponds

5

Public Car Park

6

Fishing Lodge

Reservoir

Bird Hide

9

1

Yew Tree Inn

Car Park

Pond

7

8

Dam Wall

Arlington

Polhill's Farm

To Berwick Station

Rowan

Distance:	7 kilometres.
Route:	From the Yew Tree Inn follow the narrow lane north eastwards to Tye Hill. Turn left and follow the road and track west to Sessingham Bridge over the Cuckmere River. Take the path leading north west and just before Sessingham Farm turn left south-westwards to Arlington Reservoir. Follow the well-marked track around the reservoir in an anti-clockwise direction past Polhill's Farm over the dam wall. Just past the end of the dam wall continue around the path until you see a sign to the bird observatory. Return back down the path and cross over the Cuckmere River to the church and car park.
Map:	OS Explorer 123: South Downs Way - Newhaven to Eastbourne.
Start / Parking:	Yew Tree Inn car park or public car park at village hall
Public Transport:	None convenient.
Conditions:	Generally flat. Track to the west of the reservoir and to the east of Sessingham Farm can be muddy at times.
Refreshments:	Yew Tree Inn is very good value.

Otter

THE WALK

Around the edges of the car park (1) at the village hall and the Yew Tree Inn you will find plants such as the **Common Mallow** and **Greater Burdock,** and in places **Buddleia** has established itself providing a feast of nectar for many butterflies in the summer.

Take the lane that leads north-eastwards past the Yew Tree Inn and up to Tye Hill.

This ancient way has hedges which at one time were "laid", a practice where the saplings of growing bushes and trees were bent at an angle of 45 degrees and woven around sticks driven into the ground.

About 20 metres up the lane on the right-hand side, look for several old **Ash** trees in the hedge whose branches grow horizontally along the hedgerow, a sure sign of hedge-laying. In late summer the ripening berries of the **Wayfaring Tree** can be seen in the hedgerow, green at first then red and finally black. Because the twigs of this tree are fibrous, easily twisted and hard to break, they are used by country people for tying up bundles.

Wayfaring Tree

A small stream crosses under the lane, its banks adorned with **Hart's Tongue** and **Male Fern.** You pass a large house "Woodborne Manor" on your left and in the spring the laneside here is full of **Primroses, Lady's Smock** and in a few places **Wood Anemone.** The **Brimstone** and **Orange Tip** butterflies are common and the **Chaffinch, Wren** and **Song Thrush** can be seen and heard.

About halfway up the lane on your right is a 5 metre-tall **Oak** tree, the remnant of one of much greater height but now with its trunk snapped off by a winter gale. Two metres up from the base you will see a neat round hole in the trunk, the nest site of a **Green Woodpecker. Common Figwort** and **Common Fleabane** grow alongside the lane, the latter being particularly attractive in late summer when its golden yellow flowers provide a feast for so many insects.

A small wood appears on your left at Tye Hill itself. At this junction turn left and follow the macadamed track westwards. You pass what was once an ancient cottage on your right but now replaced with one of modern design. About 400 metres down this track on the left you come to Raylands Farm (2). Here the macadam ends and the track narrows to a footpath. Just beyond the farm and on your right amongst the trees and bushes look for the 70 centimetre-tall evergreen shrub called **Butcher's Broom.** The dark green sharply pointed leaves are really flattened branches, the true leaves being reduced to small scales on the stem. The tiny greenish-white flowers appear from January to April to be followed in May and October by bright red berries. At one time butchers found the prickly "leaves" ideal for cleaning chopping blocks.

Spindle Trees grow in a number of places along this way and in the autumn they are adorned with the bright pink, four-lobed fruits which birds find so irresistible. The spindle tree was so named because for centuries it was used by womenfolk (known as spinsters) for spindles to spin wool, its wood being hard, smooth and kind to the fingers. The **Early Purple Orchid** grows on the banks beside the path in April and May together with Primroses and Bluebells. The Early Purple Orchid was first mentioned by Shakespeare in Hamlet as "Long Purples" in his description of Ophelia's death garland. He also referred to them as "dead men's fingers", a reference to the shape of their tubers. You are sure to see **Long-tailed Tits** here, particularly in the autumn and winter months, when they are joined by **Redwings** and **Fieldfares** seeking **Hawthorn** and **Blackthorn** berries.

Soon you see ahead the wooden bridge across the Cuckmere River, known as Sessingham Bridge (3). Just before you reach it there is an opening in the hedgerow to your right and a notice depicting Sessingham Moat just across the adjoining field.

This is an ancient place mentioned in the Domesday Book and is worth exploring particularly in May when the warblers have just arrived from Africa. The **Blackcap** is one that you should recognise easily, the male having a glossy black crown down to eye-level and the female with a red-brown crown. The Blackcap likes to sing its rich warbling song from the top of the tall bushes that flourish in this area. At the same time you will probably hear the distinctive bubbling "chook-chook-chook" and a slow "piu-piu-piu" of the **Nightingale,** which you are unlikely to see because it is shy and sings from the deep thicket within the confines of the moat itself. The moat is a deep defensive ditch often filled to overflowing with water. It is bordered on its western edge by the Cuckmere and the site of what was once an important habitation is now covered with tall **Ash, Alder** and **Willow.** Ancient trees lie fallen and rotting everywhere and with extreme care it is possible to gain access to the thicket-covered mound in the middle. However, nothing remains of the great house that once existed here, except for a few pieces of old brick. The Domesday Book reveals that the tithe for Sessingham and the watermill on the opposite bank of the river, was 500 eels a year. Two thousand years ago the moat and the mound within it could well have been a Roman camp.

Before returning to Sessingham Bridge, pause awhile here and feel the history of the place. The presence of wild **Hops** trailing over nearby bushes gives an indication that they were once cultivated and used locally by brewers to clarify beer and to give it a bitter flavour.

Back at the bridge look to the left of the path just before crossing the river and you will find the **Common Hemp-nettle** with very pale pink flowers which appear in August and September. On the river bank you will see the two metre-tall reddish stems and large purple-pink flowers of **Indian Balsam.** This is also called **Jumping Jacks** or **Policeman's Helmet** and was introduced to gardens from the Himalayas in 1839. Since then it has spread widely and dominates areas of river bank throughout Britain flowering from July to October. The seeds and seed pods can be eaten and have a pleasant nutty flavour. Also growing here and flowering in July and August

Indian Balsam

is the **Purple Loosestrife** with its dense spikes of reddish-purple flowers on metre-tall stems. Loosestrife is a literal translation from a Greek name for the plant. At the time of the classical Greek civilisation this plant was believed to be so powerful that it was draped around the yoke of quarrelling oxen to calm them down. Floating on the surface of the gently flowing Cuckmere here are **Broad-leaved Pondweed** and the **Yellow Water-lily** with its large, flat and rounded leaves.

Walk a little way on the path alongside the western edge of the river. This is a quiet undisturbed place where the only noise will be the hum of bees and the gentle whirring of fast flying **Dragonflies.** Sit quietly on the bank here in spring and summer and you may be rewarded by the blue flash, like an electric spark, of a **Kingfisher** flying along the river. If you are lucky you may see it suddenly hover and then plunge into the water after its prey of small fish. The birds make their nests in holes bored about one metre deep in the river bank just above the water level.

The **Otter** was once a relatively common creature of Sussex rivers some 50 years ago but pollution from herbicides and the escape of the aggressive **American Mink** from fur farms has brought about its extinction. However in recent years conservationists have re-introduced it to some Hampshire and Sussex rivers and their success can be measured by the spread of this shy and delightful mammal across the south. So it is just possible that you may catch sight of the otter on quiet stretches of the Cuckmere near Sessingham especially in the evening or early morning. The **Mink** is fairly common on the river here but is easily recognised, being much smaller than the otter with a tail only 15 centimetres long as opposed to 47 centimetres long in the case of the otter.

After a long dry spell the river at Sessingham Bridge can become quite shallow and just to the north the muddy banks become exposed. Here you may see the **Common Sandpiper** feeding particularly in August when small parties are returning south on passage. As they are disturbed listen to their shrill piping "Twee-see-see".

The path beyond Sessingham Bridge can become muddy after heavy rain and almost impassable if the Cuckmere floods, which it often does. In spring there are a variety of wild flowers to see, **Primroses, Greater Stitchwort, Lady's Smock** and **Early Purple Orchid.** The **Brimstone** and **Orange Tip** butterflies should be seen together with the **Wren** and **Blackbird.** In May the warblers begin to arrive and you will hear the **Chiffchaff** and the **Cuckoo.**

As you walk up this leafy track note the small stream on your left and the deep indentation in the field on your right which was once the ancient mill pond. Some 300 metres up the track from Sessingham Bridge and 80 metres before a macadamed lane you turn left across a small bridge over the stream. This turning point is marked by tall oak trees with a green sign, somewhat hidden by undergrowth on your right, which says "To Arlington Reservoir". As you cross the bridge look for the **Lesser Periwinkle** *growing on the banks. The violet-blue flowers appear in March and April. As you emerge from the trees and shrubs look to your right at a small cottage which was once a farm worker's house (4).*

It was empty and derelict for many years at the end of the last century but just recently it has been restored and is now inhabited. A year ago a large old barn still stood attached to the north side of the cottage. This was once used as a winter shelter for bullocks and as a place to stack sheaves of wheat before threshing. Early in the last century threshing was accomplished with flails, the wheat grains being swept up from the floor after winnowing, and the chaff and straw swept out into the yard as fodder for the hungry bullocks. The barn has recently been converted and is now part of the cottage itself. A tall **Copper Beech** and a **Scots Pine** still grow in the garden planted by a Mr Blackwell in the 19th century and the old mill stones from Sessingham watermill are still said to exist nearby, concreted into the floor of what was once a pigsty.

A sense of history still pervades over this place and in the spring **Snowdrops** and **Daffodils** give colour to grassy banks here, although there are not nearly so many of them now, as before the old cottage was restored.

The path leads south-westwards past the back of the cottage where a large pond surrounded with **Great Reedmace** still gives shelter to a pair of **Moorhens.** On the other side of the pond and to the north are the old buildings of Sessingham Farm itself now used for storage. Two tall **White Willows** dominate this old farmyard; the white down under their leaves giving them a striking silvery appearance when the wind stirs their foliage.

The path to the reservoir is bordered by an old hedgerow on its northern flank with tall **Oaks** and smaller shrubs of **Dog Rose, Honeysuckle, Blackthorn, Elder** and **Hazel.** Birds like the **Wren, Chaffinch, Long-tailed Tit** and **Yellowhammer** find good cover here for their nests. In the surrounding cultivated fields grow plants like **Small-flowered Cranesbill, Scarlet Pimpernel, Marsh Cudweed, Field Pansy, Perennial Sow-thistle** and **Common Field Speedwell.** The best time to see these wildflowers is in late summer after the cereal crops have been cut and harvested.

The path leads gently uphill to the edge of the large wooded area that was planted with 30,000 native trees and shrubs on the northern edge of Arlington Reservoir after it was completed in 1971. You pass through a gate and are then surrounded by bushes of **Hawthorn, Hazel** and **Blackthorn** interspersed with trees of **Ash, Rowan, Birch, Oak** and **Wild Cherry.** *The path soon opens out on your right with good views of open fields and countryside. Some 100 metres past the gate you come to a path that joins from the left and has a green sign pointing to the left stating "Public Footpath" (5). If you want to take a shorter route and do not wish to walk all the way around the reservoir, then follow this public footpath that leads to the Osprey Bird Hide and to the northern edge of the dam wall.*

If you have the time and energy, follow the path marked "Bridleway" which soon opens out to give glorious views of Arlington Reservoir itself and the distant escarpment of the South Downs with Bostal Hill prominent, together with the chalkpit at Bo Peep.

Some 250 metres from point 5 the path forks. Take the left fork marked "Public Footpath" which takes you beside the water and through the grass meadow.

This meadow was specially planted as a haven for butterflies of which 35 different species have been recorded. In the late spring and summer you should see many of these, including the **Small Tortoiseshell** and **Red Admiral.** There is a good colony of **Marbled Whites** here and in a good year you will see the **Clouded Yellow** flying fast across the tall grasses. In August and September the meadow is awash with **Common Fleabane** and **Ragwort,** their yellow flowers contrasting well with the grey-brown and green grasses and the sparkling blue of the reservoir waters. Two reed-fringed ponds are worth exploring just to the north of the public car park (6). These provide a source of mud for **Swallows** and **House Martins** to build their nests.

In front of the car park is the bird feeding area where **Canada Geese** and **Mallard** are remarkably tame and feed from your hand. In front of you are reedbeds of **Common Reed Grass** in which **Reed** and **Sedge Warblers** build their nests. At this place you will see many of the 173 recorded species of bird including the **Pied Wagtail, Common Sandpiper, Great Crested Grebe** and **Cormorant** but the best place to observe the birds are at the Osprey Bird Hide later in the walk.

Common Fleabane

Follow the well marked path in front of the fishing lodge and beside the waters edge. Just before you reach the group of buildings making up Polhill's Farm look for a large pond which has a pond-dipping platform (7).

This pond was enlarged by South East Water in 1999 to form an aquatic environment for microscopic organisms. Insects such as **Dragonflies, Pond Skaters** and **Water Boatmen,** together with amphibians such as **Frogs** and **Great Crested Newts** all thrive here, and in turn these attract birds like the **Grey Heron** and **Kingfisher.**

The path diverts around the farm which was once the site of a large Roman pottery and soon you are onto the dam wall itself (8).

This part of the walk is very exposed and the wind can be strong at times, often blowing across the open waters and causing waves to crash ashore amongst spumes of white foam. Windover Hill is prominent to your right and the ageless Giant looks down upon you impassively and with cold aloofness. Many plants grow between the cracks in the dam wall at or near the waters edge, and particularly in summer when the water is low, you will find **Marsh Woundwort, Gipsywort** and **Silverweed.** The ground-hugging leaves of the last named plant, with their colour of silky green above and matt grey beneath are common everywhere on your walk wherever it is damp. They form downy mats beside pathways and in waste places and from June to August they are spangled with bright yellow five-petalled flowers. Like **Mugwort,** the leaves of silverweed are believed to give comfort to travellers if stuffed inside their shoes. Silverweed roots were once cultivated in the poorer parts of upland Britain and eaten, being first baked and then dried and ground into flour. Silverweed was eaten right up to the end of the nineteenth century in the Scottish Highlands particularly in times of famine.

As you walk over the dam and look across at the 49 hectares of open reservoir containing some three and a half million litres of water, it is hard to imagine that this was once an area of cultivation enclosed within a meander of the Cuckmere River. Now with the help of South East Water and English Nature it is a wonderful nature reserve and site of special scientific interest (S.S.S.I.).

Soon you reach the northern edge of the dam wall when on your right you will see a notice board describing the reservoir and its abundant wildlife. Continue north-westwards along the path through the scrub for about 80 metres until you see a sign "Bird Hide" directing you down a path to your left.

Before you arrive at this point, however, look and listen, particularly where the path opens out slightly. The grassy edges abound with wild flowers and in May and June the sound of many birds will be heard, **Blackcaps, Whitethroats, Willow Warblers, Garden Warblers, Nightingales** and **Chiffchaffs** amongst them. If you remain quiet and still your patience will be rewarded by seeing some of them.

At the Osprey Bird Hide be prepared to rest awhile for here is the best place to view the abundant birdlife.

Around the inside of the hide are illustrations of many of the bird species you are likely to see. Some 173 different birds have been recorded, one of the highlights being the **Osprey.** These large birds of prey arrive in this country from Africa in April and May on their migration, and return in August and September. In the 1970's an Osprey platform was erected just to the north-west of the hide and every year several birds are seen eating **Rainbow Trout** caught in the reservoir on or near the platform. They then make their way north to their breeding grounds in northern England, Scotland and Scandinavia. One day, perhaps, they will remain at Arlington to feed on the large supply of fish and to nest in the tall trees of Abbot's Wood and Friston Forest. The end of April, early May and late August and September is a good time to see the Osprey.

An hour or so in the hide with a pair of binoculars should reveal many birds, some of which will undoubtedly be new to the amateur naturalist. In addition to those already mentioned, you may see the **Common Tern** making a splash as it dives steeply into the water for fish, the **Black Tern** skimming fast across the surface and the **Green Sandpiper** flying along the water's edge. Others you may see include the many species of duck, like the **Widgeon, Pochard, Tufted** and **Shoveller.** For the expert bird spotter you may be lucky and see varieties such as the **Great Northern Diver** or **Temminck's Stint.** For reasons that must be obvious, probably the best time to view birds at the reservoir is during the spring and autumn migration but you will still enjoy good sightings at any time of the year.

As you return back to the dam wall, you will see the **Speckled Wood** butterfly flitting about sun-dappled patches beside the path and as you reach the dam wall itself you may see some of the many dragonflies that abound in the area such as the **Emperor** (the largest in Britain), **Hairy** and **Common Aeshna.**

Just beside the notice board which you saw earlier, cross over a stile that leads across a grassy field to Arlington Parish Church.

This field was once too heavily grazed but in recent years the livestock have been controlled and the grass is now long enough perhaps for **Skylarks** and **Meadow Pipits** to return. Nearby is an area fenced off, where nature has been allowed to take its course and where scrub and trees grow through very tall lush grass, an ideal habitat for rodents of many kinds to flourish. These provide a good source of food for **Barn Owls.** There are now some 30 nesting boxes suitable for barn owls or **Kestrels** in the Cuckmere Valley and those near the reservoir have been very successful. So at dusk, as the sun sets behind the distant hills, you may see this wraith-like owl fly gracefully with slow silent wingbeats across the grassy meadow. As it quarters the area, suddenly you see it close its wings and drop down to earth to pounce on a small unsuspecting field mouse.

In late April, **Yellow Wagtails** are often seen on the grassy banks of the dam wall as they arrive from Africa. Fifty years ago these were fairly common breeding birds in the Cuckmere Valley but with the increase in intensive farming and the drainage of lush water meadows they seldom nest in the area. However, small flocks of them are seen in the spring at Arlington Reservoir and with good management of nearby water meadows perhaps they will once again remain to breed successfully.

You cross the Cuckmere at a modern bridge just 200 metres south of Arlington Church. As you cross look down at the river bank and see patches of **Purple Loosestrife**. On the water itself the bright yellow flowers of the **Yellow Water-lily** are easily seen and beside the bridge itself grows the **Common Mallow.** Beyond this bridge the path crosses a field and then you turn left over a small stream by way of another smaller bridge and a stile. The church of St. Pancras stands proud before you, sheltered by **Yew** and **Horse Chestnut** trees. This must be one of the oldest of Sussex churches and it stands on the site of a remote pagan cemetery where Bronze Age urns with human ashes were once dug up. Nearby, a wide patch of water on the Cuckmere is called Bell Hole. Some connect this with Bel or Baal, the sungod of ancient peoples, which itself could be associated with the great figure that looks down from Windover Hill. A fitting place to conclude the walks around the Cuckmere Valley for *the car park where you started this last walk is but a 100 metres down the road from the church.*

Purple Loosestrife

Barn Owl

EPILOGUE

I thought it fitting to conclude this book of wanderings over a small but beautiful part of the British countryside with quotations from two of our greatest poets.

First from Evening: Ponte al Mare, Pisa, by Percy Bysshe Shelley and, although describing a place well distant from the Cuckmere, it has a certain empathy:

> *The sun is set, the swallows are asleep;*
> *The bats are flitting fast in the grey air;*
> *The slow soft toads out of damp corners creep,*
> *And evening's breath, wandering here and there*
> *Over the quivering surface of the stream,*
> *Wakes not one ripple from its summer dream.*
>
> *There is no dew on the dry grass to-night,*
> *Nor damp within the shadow of the trees;*
> *The wind is intermitting, dry, and light;*
> *And in the inconstant motion of the breeze*
> *The dust and straws are driven up and down,*
> *And whirled about the pavement of the town.*

Secondly, from one of William Wordsworth's sonnets:

> *The world is too much with us; late and soon,*
> *Getting and spending, we lay waste our powers:*
> *Little we see in nature that is ours;*
> *We have given our hearts away, a sordid boon!*

Hopefully, having walked these paths you will have seen a good deal of nature that is ours and which is so much a part of our great heritage.

P.C.

BIBLIOGRAPHY

AA Book of Britain's Countryside .... Midsummer Books 1998

Coulcher, Patrick *A Natural History of the Cuckmere Valley* ..... The Book Guild 1997

Coulcher, Patrick *Unto the Hills - The History and Wildlife of the South Downs*
.... The Book Guild 2001

*Mitchell, Alan; and Wilkinson, John *The Trees of Britain and Northern Europe*
.... Collins 1982

*Peterson, Roger;Mountford, Guy and Hollom P.A.D. *A Field Guide to the Birds of Britain and Europe* .... Collins 1954

*Phillips, Roger *Grasses, Ferns, Mosses and Lichens of Great Britain and Ireland*
.... Macmillan 1980

*Phillips, Roger *Mushrooms and Other Fungi of Great Britain and Europe* ....
.... New Interinth 1981

*Readers Digest *Field Guide to the Butterflies and Other Insects of Britain* ....
.... Macmillan 1984

*Rose, Francis *The Wild Flower Key - British Isles, N.W. Europe* ...Frederick Warne 1981

*Streeter, David and Garrard, Ian *The Wild Flowers of the British Isles* ....
.... Midsummer Books 1983

* These are useful books for identification purposes

INDEX

Animals, Ferns, Fungi, Insects, Trees, Shrubs and others
Bold numbers refer to pages with illustrations

	Months Seen
London Plane 27	Jan - Dec
M	
Maidenhair Spleenwort 32	Jan - Dec
Male Fern 73, 82, 86	Jan - Dec
Many-zoned Polypore 82	Jan - Dec
Marl Pit 71	Jan - Dec
Mink 88	Jan - Dec
Mullet 20	Jan - Dec
N	
Norway Maple 27	Jan - Dec
O	
Oak 73, 80, 81, 82, 86, 89	Jan - Dec
Osier Willow 79, 82	Jan - Dec
Otter **85,** 88	Jan - Dec
Oyster Mushroom 82	
P	
Parasol Mushroom **34,** 34	Jun - Oct
Pendulous Sedge 73	Jan - Dec
Pond Skater 90	Mar - Sep
Privet 70	Jan - Dec
Puffball 13	Aug - Sep
Q	
Quaking Grass 38	
R	
Rabbit 39	Jan - Dec
Radiolaria 14	
Rainbow Trout 91	Jan - Dec
Roe Deer **76,** 81	Jan - Dec
Rowan 70, **84,** 89	Jan - Dec
S	
Scarlet Hood 34	Aug - Oct
Scots Pine 12, 24, 81, 89	Jan - Dec
Silver Birch 78, 81, 82, 89	Jan - Dec
Soil Creep 64	Jan - Dec
Southern Hawker 33	May - Oct
Spindle Tree 86	Jan - Dec
Stoat 33	Jan - Dec

	Months Seen
Stinkhorn **58,** 82	Jul - Nov
Sulphur Tuft 13, 82	Sep - Nov
Sweet Chestnut 81	Jan - Dec
Sycamore 49, 65, 70	Jan - Dec
T	
Tor Grass 47, 63	Jan - Dec
U	
Upright Brome 38	Jan - Dec
W	
Wall-rue 32	Jan - Dec
Water Boatman 90	Mar - Sep
Wayfaring Tree 32, 38, 40, 48, 70, **86,** 86	Jan - Dec
Weasel **33,** 33	Jan - Dec
Weeping Elm 32	Jan - Dec
Western Hemlock 81	Jan - Dec
White Willow 89	Jan - Dec
Wild Cherry 24, 89	Jan - Dec
Willow 87	Jan - Dec
Wood Ant 79	Jan - Dec
Y	
Yellow Hill Ant 40	Jan - Dec
Yew 24, 92	Jan - Dec

Birds

	Months Seen			Months Seen
			Grey Heron 19, 90	Jan - Dec
B				
Barn Owl 65, 91, **92**	Jan - Dec		**H**	
Blackbird 65, 73, 88	Jan - Dec		Hedge Sparrow 48, 73	Jan - Dec
Blackcap 27, 35, 82, 87, 91	Apr - Oct		Herring Gull 19	Jan - Dec
Black-headed Gull 19	Jan - Dec		Hobby 20, **22,** 26	Apr - Oct
Black Tern 91	May - Oct		House Martin 63, 90	Apr - Oct
Blue Tit 78	Jan - Dec		House Sparrow 73	Jan - Dec
Brent Goose 19	Sep - Apr			
Buzzard 72	Mar - Oct		**J**	
			Jay 26, 27, **28,** 79	Jan - Dec
C				
Canada Goose 19, **57,** 79, 90	Jan - Dec		**K**	
Chaffinch 21, 26, 27, 33, 41, 74, 86, 89	Jan - Dec		Kestrel **39,** 39, 71, 91	Jan - Dec
Chiffchaff 18, 20, 50, 81, 88, 91	Mar - Sep		Kingfisher 11, 19, 88, 90, **Back cover**	Jan - Dec
Collared Dove 80	Jan - Dec			
Common Gull 19	Jul - Jan		**L**	
Common Sandpiper 19, 88, 90	Apr - Sep		Lapwing 19, **72,** 72	Jan - Dec
Common Tern 91	Apr - Sep		Lesser Whitethroat 35	Apr - Sep
Cormorant 90	Jan - Dec		Linnet 27, 32, 48, 65, 71	Jan - Dec
Corn Bunting 40	Jan - Dec		Little Egret 11, 19	Jan - Dec
Crow 19	Jan - Dec		Long-tailed Tit **12,** 12, 78, 87, 89	Jan - Dec
Cuckoo 64, 88, 73	Apr - Aug			
			M	
D			Magpie 27, 49	Jan - Dec
Dunlin 19	Jul - May		Mallard 19, 79, 90	Jan - Dec
			Martins 20, 63	Mar - Sep
F			Meadow Pipit 10, 40, 62, 91	Jan - Dec
Fieldfare 87	Oct - Mar		Mistle Thrush 26, 33	Jan - Dec
Fulmar Petrel **8,** 10, **51**	Jan - Aug		Moorhen 74, 79, 89	Jan - Dec
			Mute Swan **69,** 72	Jan - Dec
G				
Garden Warbler 27, 35, 82, 91	Apr - Sep		**N**	
Godwit 19	Jul - Apr		Nightingale 20, **30,** 35, 82, 87, 91	Apr - Sep
Goldcrest **76,** 78	Jan - Dec		Nightjar 81	May - Oct
Goldfinch **42,** 42	Jan - Dec		Nuthatch **56,** 80	Jan - Dec
Great Crested Grebe 90	Jan - Dec			
Great Northern Diver 91	Dec - Apr		**O**	
Great Spotted Woodpecker 26, 78, 79	Jan - Dec		Osprey 91, **104**	Apr - May, Aug - Sep
Great Tit 78	Jan - Dec			
Greenfinch 26, 27	Jan - Dec		**P**	
Green Sandpiper 91	Jul - Sep		Partridge 71	Jan - Dec
Green Woodpecker **26,** 40, 46, 86	Jan - Dec			

Birds

	Months Seen		Months Seen
Peregrine Falcon **16,** 19	Jan - Dec	**Y**	
Pheasant **36,** 38, 44	Jan - Dec	Yaffle **26,** 27	Jan - Aug
Pied Wagtail 90	Jan - Dec	Yellowhammer 21, 33, 65, 74, 89	Jan - Dec
Pochard 19, 91	Sep - Mar	Yellow Wagtail 92	Apr - Sep

R

	Months Seen
Redshank 11, 19	Jan - Dec
Redwing 87	Oct - Apr
Reed Bunting 20, 73	Jan - Dec
Reed Warbler 20, 72, 90	Apr - Sep
Robin 65, 73, 74	Jan - Dec
Rock Pipit 14	Jan - Dec
Rook 19, **36,** 38	Jan - Dec

S

Sand Martin 63	Mar - Sep
Sandpiper 19, 90	Apr - Sep
Sedge Warbler 20, 72, 90	Apr - Oct
Shelduck 11	Jan - Dec
Shoveller 91	Jan - Dec
Skylark 10, 26, **28,** 39, 40, 62, 91	Jan - Dec
Snipe **68,** 71	Jan - Dec
Song Thrush 73, 86	Jan - Dec
Sparrowhawk **71,** 71	Jan - Dec
Stonechat 11, 66	Jan - Dec
Swallow 20, 63, 90	Mar - Oct

T

Temminck's Stint 91	
Tufted Duck 19, 91	Jan - Dec
Turtle Dove **49,** 80	Apr - Sep

W

Wheatear 3, 18	Apr - Aug
Whitethroat 18, 27, 32, 33, 48, 50, 71, 74, 82, 91	Apr - Sep
Widgeon 19, 91	Sep - Mar
Willow Warbler **18,** 18, 20, 33, 34, 50, 91	Apr - Sep
Woodcock 66	Jan - Dec
Wood Pigeon 46	Jan - Dec
Wren 35, 73, 74, 86, 88, 89	Jan - Dec

Butterflies and Moths

	Months on Wing
A	
Adonis 40, 50	May - Jun, Aug - Sep
B	
Brimstone 38, 48, 64, 86, 88	Apr - Jun, Aug - Sep
Brown Argus 47	May - Jun, Aug - Sep
C	
Chalkhill Blue 47, 48, 50, **55**, 66	Jul - Aug,
Clouded Yellow **56,** 89	Jun - Sep
Comma 24, 46, **55**, 64	Apr - May, Jul - Sep
Common Blue 25, 33, 38, 47, **56,** 66	May - Jun, Aug - Sep
D	
Dark Green Fritillary 35, 47	Jun - Aug
Dingy Skipper 47, 50, 66	Apr - Jun, Aug
E	
Essex Skipper 40, 50	Jul - Aug
G	
Gatekeeper 47, 66	Jul - Aug
Grayling 34, 40	Jul - Aug
Green Hairstreak 20, 35	Jun - Jul
Green-veined White 47, 74	Apr - Sep
Grizzled Skipper 34, 47, 72	May - Jun, Aug
L	
Large Skipper 33, 40, 47, 50	Jun - Aug
Large White 47	Apr - Oct
M	
Marbled White 33, 47, 66, 89	Jul - Aug
Meadow Brown 19, 25, 33, 38, 47, 66, 78	Jun - Aug
O	
Orange Tip 19, 28, 41, 48, **54,** 64, 86, 88	Apr - Jun

	Months on Wing
P	
Painted Lady 24, 27, 46, 47	Jul - Aug
Peacock 24, 27, 41, 46, 47, 48, 49	Apr - May, Aug - Sep
R	
Red Admiral 27, 40, 46, 48, 49, **52,** 78, 89	Jul - Sep
Ringlet 50, 78	Jul - Aug
S	
Silver-spotted Skipper 40, **53**	Jul - Aug
Silver-washed Fritillary 78	Jul - Aug
Six-spot Burnet Moth 48, 50	Jun - Jul
Small Blue 47	May - Jun, Aug
Small Copper 33, 47, 72, 73, 78	Apr - May, Aug - Sep
Small Heath 66	
Small Skipper 33, 40, 47, 50, **53,** 66	Jun - Aug
Small Tortoiseshell 19, 38, 40, 41, 46, 89, **Back cover**	Jul - Aug
Small White 47	Apr - Sep
Speckled Wood 28, 46, 47, 49, **54,** 78, 91	Apr - Sep
W	
Wall Brown 46, 47, 48	May, Jul - Sep
White Admiral 81	Jun - Aug
White-letter Hairstreak 20	

Wild Flowers

Months in Flower

A

Adonis 24	Jun - Jul
Agrimony 46, 66	Jun - Jul
Alexanders 70	
Annual Sea-blite 21	Jul - Sep
Aquilegia 72	May - Jun
Autumn Gentian 33, 39	Jul - Sep
Autumn Lady's-tresses Orchid **56,** 66	Aug - Sep

B

Basil Thyme 20	May - Sep
Bee Orchid 40, 41, **43,** 66, **Back cover**	Jun - Jul
Bell Heather 34, 39	Jul - Sep
Bird's-foot Trefoil 13, 35, 47, 65	Apr - Sep
Bitter-cress 19	Apr - Aug
Black Horehound 49	Jul - Sep
Bluebell 12, 73, 78, 81	Apr - May
Branched Bur-reed 13, 33	Jun - Aug
Bristly Oxtongue 14	Jun - Nov
Broad-leaved Garlic 32	Apr - Jun
Broad-leaved Helleborine 24	Jul - Sep
Broad-leaved Pondweed 88	May - Sep
Brooklime 71	May - Aug
Bucks-horn Plantain 21	Jul - Sep
Bullrush 13	Jun - Jul
Burdock 12, 40	Jul - Sep
Burnet Rose 47	May - Jul
Burnt Orchid 41, **54**	Jun - Aug
Butcher's Broom 86	Jan - Oct

C

Calamint 20	Jul - Sep
Carline Thistle 24, 39, 47, 62, 66	Jul - Sep
Celery-leaved Buttercup 20	May - Sep
Chicory 35	Jun - Sep
Clematis 24, 46, 49	Jul - Aug
Clustered Bellflower 18	Jun - Oct
Codlins-and-cream 79	Jul - Aug
Common Centaury 33, 47, 48, 62	Jul - Aug
Common Comfrey 71	May - Jun
Common Field Speedwell 89	Jan - Dec
Common Figwort 86	Jun - Sep

Months in Flower

Common Fleabane 73, 78, 86, **90,** 90	Jul - Sep
Common Knapweed 32, 65	Jun - Sep
Common Hemp-nettle 74, 87	Jul - Sep
Common Mallow 21, 62, 65, 86, 92	Jun - Jul
Common Poppy 35, 49, 62	Apr - Aug
Common Restharrow 62	Jun - Sep
Common Rock-rose **30,** 32, 35, 38, 48	May - Sep
Common Spotted Orchid 38, 41, **42,** 62, 63, 66, 73, 79, 80, 81	Jun - Jul
Common Toadflax 35	Jun - Oct
Common Twayblade Orchid 38, 41	May - Jul
Cow Parsley 70	Apr - Jun
Cowslip **8,** 11, 18, 70	Apr - Jun
Creeping Cinquefoil 71	May - Aug
Crosswort 41	Apr - Jun
Cuckoo Flower **64,** 64	Apr - Jun

D

Daffodil 32, 89	Mar - May
Dame's-violet 72	May - Aug
Deadly Nightshade 46	Aug - Oct
Devil's-bit Scabious 79	Jun - Oct
Dog Rose 70, 89	Jun - Jul
Dove's-foot Cranesbill 24, 47, 49, 62	Apr - Sep
Dwarf Centaury 18	Apr - Sep
Dwarf Spurge 65	May - Sep

E

Early Dog-violet 38	Feb - May
Early Forget-me-not 40	Mar - Apr
Early Purple Orchid 32, **58,** 65, 87, 88	Apr - May
Early Spider Orchid 11, **51**	Apr - May
Elecampane **58,** 64	Jun - Sep
Enchanter's Nightshade 81	Jun - Sep
Eyebright 33, 47, 63, 65	Jun - Oct

F

Felwort 39, 47	Jul - Sep
Field Fleawort 10	May
Field Gentian 39	Sep - Oct
Field Gromwell 35	May - Jul
Field Pansy 35, 49, 62, 89	Apr - Nov

Wild Flowers

	Months in Flower
Field Scabious 32, 38, 47, 49, 65	Jul - Sep
Fine-leaved Water Dropwort 74	Jun - Aug
Flowering Rush 20	Jul - Sep
Fragrant Orchid 38, 63, 66, **67**	Jun - Jul
Fringed Water-lily **57**, 80	Jun - Aug
Frogbit 20	Jul - Aug
Frog Orchid 35, 41	Jul - Aug

G

Garlic Mustard 19	Apr - Jul
Germander Speedwell 27, **51**	May - Jul
Gipsywort 78, 79, 90	Jul - Aug
Gladdon 18	May - Jun
Goat's Beard 46	Jun - Jul
Greater Burdock 86	Jul - Sep
Greater Butterfly Orchid 64	May - Jul
Greater Knapweed 65	Jun - Aug
Greater Sea-spurrey 20	Jun - Sep
Greater Spearwort 13, 80	Jun - Sep
Greater Stitchwort 74, 88	Apr - Jun
Great Mullein 12, 40	Jun - Aug
Great Reedmace 13, **31**, 33, 71, 89	Jun - Jul
Great Willowherb 49, **60**, 65, 79	Jul - Aug
Ground Ivy 18	Mar - May

H

Hairy Violet 12, 18, 32, 35, 47	Mar - May
Harebell 41, 50	Jul - Sep
Hedge Woundwort 79	Jul - Sep
Hemlock 70	Jun - Jul
Hemlock Water-dropwort 74	Jun - Jul
Hemp Agrimony 27, 47, 48, 49	Jul - Sep
Henbane 18	Jun - Aug
Herb Robert 74	Apr - Sep
Hogweed 46	Jun - Jul
Honeysuckle 49, 73, 81, 89	May - Jun
Horseshoe Vetch 47, 62	May - Jul
Hound's-tongue 14	Jun - Aug

I

Indian Balsam **87**, 87	Jul - Oct

	Months in Flower
J	
Jumping Jack **87**, 87	Jul - Aug
K	
Kidney Vetch 18, 25, 47, 65	Jun - Sep
Knapweed 35	Jun - Jul
L	
Lady's Bedstraw 41, 50, 62	Jul - Aug
Lady's Mantle 80	Jun - Sep
Lady's Smock 19, **64**, 64, 73, 86, 88	Apr - Jun
Large Bindweed 46	Jul - Aug
Large White Helleborine 26, **52**	May - Jun
Lesser Burdock 26	Jul - Sep
Lesser Celandine 13, 73	Apr - May
Lesser Centaury 48	Jul - Aug
Lesser Hawkbit 48	Jun - Sep
Lesser Periwinkle 88	Mar - May
Lesser Sea-spurrey 20	Jun - Sep
Lesser Scullcap 82	Jul - Oct
Lesser Spearwort 73, **78**, 79, 81	May - Sep
Ling 34	Jul - Sep
Lousewort 82	Apr - Aug
M	
Marjoram 46	Jun - Jul
Marsh Cudweed 89	Jul - Sep
Marsh Woundwort 72, 90	Jul - Sep
Meadow Buttercup 71	May - Aug
Milk Thistle **21**, 21	Jun - Jul
Moon Carrot 19	Jul - Aug
Moschatel **31**, 32, 41	Mar - Apr
Moth Mullein **53**, 72	Jun - Sep
Mountain Stone Parsley 19	Jul - Aug
Mugwort 46, 48, 90	Jul - Sep
Musk Mallow **56**, 81	Jul - Aug
Musk Thistle **55**, 66	May - Aug
N	
Narrow-leaved Bird's-foot Trefoil 14	Jun - Aug
O	
Old Man's Beard 24, 46	Jul - Aug

Wild Flowers

	Months in Flower
P	
Parsley Piert 72	Apr - Oct
Pepperwort 18	May - Aug
Perforate St John's-wort 46	Jun - Sep
Perennial Sow-thistle 46, 89	Jul - Oct
Pheasant's-eye 24	Jun - Jul
Pineappleweed 62	May - Nov
Pink 63	Jul - Aug
Ploughman's Spikenard 24	Jul - Sep
Policeman's Helmet **87,** 87	Jul - Oct
Pride of Sussex 39	Jul - Aug
Primrose 38, 73, 86, 88	Apr - May
Purple Loosetrife 72, 88, **92**	Aug - Sep
Pyramidal Orchid **60,** 63, **67**	Jul - Aug
R	
Ragged Robin 71, 73	May - Aug
Ragwort 90	Jun - Oct
Ramsons 32	Apr - Jun
Red Bartsia 46	Jun - Aug
Red Campion 73	Mar - Oct
Red Star-thistle 20, **52**	Jul - Aug
Roast-beef Plant 18	May - Jun
Rock Sea Lavender 14	Jul - Sep
Rosebay Willowherb 25, 50, 62, 80	Jul - Sep
Round-headed Rampion 39, 47	Jul - Aug
Round-leaved Fluellen 49, 65	Jul - Oct
S	
Salad Burnet 24, 25, 34, 63, 65	May - Aug
Scarlet Pimpernel 46, 49, 89	Jun - Aug
Scentless Mayweed 14	Jul - Sep
Sea Aster 21	Jul - Sep
Sea Beet 21	Jul - Sep
Sea-heath 21	Jul - Aug
Sea Pink 18	Apr - Jul
Sea Purslane 21	Jul - Sep
Sea Stork's-bill 10	May - Sep
Selfheal 25, **55,** 80	Jul - Oct
Sharp-leaved Fluellen 35, 49	Jul - Oct
Sheep's Sorrel 72	May - Jun
Silverweed 73, 74, 90	Jun - Aug

	Months in Flower
Skullcap 80, 82	Jun - Sep
Slender Speedwell 27	May - Jun
Slender St John's-wort 48	Jun - Aug
Small-flowered Cranesbill 89	Jun - Sep
Small Scabious 38, 47, **50,** 50, 65	Jul - Sep
Smooth Hawk's-beard 48	Jun - Sep
Snowdrop 12, 32, 89	Feb - Mar
Southern Marsh Orchid 73	Jun - Jul
Spiked Rampion **57,** 78, 80	May - Jun
Spiny Restharrow 41, 62	Jun - Sep
Spring Whitlow-grass 40	Mar - Apr
Spurge Laurel 28, 38	Feb - Apr
Squinancywort 66	Jun - Jul
Stinking Iris 18	May - Jun
Stonecrop 14	Jul - Aug
Strawberry Clover 20	May - Jun
Subterranean Clover 72	May - Jun
Sweet Violet 70	Feb - May
T	
Tall Melilot 50, 65	Jun - Aug
Tamarisk 13	Jul - Sep
Thrift 18	Apr - Jul
Thistles 35	Jun - Jul
Tormentil 34	Jun - Sep
Town Hall Clock **31,** 32	Mar - Apr
Traveller's Joy 24	Jul - Aug
Twayblade Orchid 63, 66	Jun - Jul
U	
Upright Hedge-parsley 46	Jul - Aug
V	
Vervain 12, 47	Jun - Sep
Viper's Bugloss 10, 34, 48	May - Oct
W	
Wall Germander 10	Jun - Sep
Wall Rocket 10	May - Sep
Water Crowfoot 20	Mar - May
Water Forget-me-not 13, 74	Jun - Aug
Water Mint 74, 81	Jul - Oct

Wild Flowers

	Months in Flower		Months in Flower
Water Plantain 20, 74	Jun -Aug	**Y**	
Water Pepper 72	Jul - Sep	Yellow Bird's-nest 12	Jun - Jul
Water Soldier 33	Jun - Aug	Yellow Iris 79	May - Jul
Weld 34, 46, 66	Jun - Sep	Yellow Pimpernel 78	May - Jun
White Horehound 20	Apr - Oct	Yellow Vetch 27	Jun - Sep
White Campion 49	May - Oct	Yellow Vetchling 27	Jun - Aug
Wild Basil 46, 48	Jul - Sep	Yellow Water-lily 72, 88, 92	Jun - Aug
Wild Carrot 46	Jun - Aug	Yellow-wort 39, **44**, 47, 63, 66	Jun - Oct
Wild Mignonette 48	Jun - Sep		
Wild Strawberry 73	Apr - Jul		
Wild Thyme 13, 32, 33, 34	May - Aug		
Wood Anemone 78, 86	Apr - May		

Illustrations of Places of Interest

A
Abbot's Wood **83**
Alfriston Church **1**
Arlington Reservoir **58**

B
Birling Gap **5, 51**
Bostal Hill **59, 66**

C
Coonatta **15**
Cradle Hill **45, 55**
Cuckmere Haven **15**
Cuckmere Valley **21, 52, 59**

D
Deep Dean **37**

F
Firle Beacon **53, 61, 66**
Floods in Cuckmere Valley **4, 59**
Folkington Church **43**
Folkington Downs **54**
Friston Forest **23, 29**

G
Green Way **59**

H
High and Over **21, 59**
Hope Gap **4**

L
Long Man of Wilmington **75**
Lynchets **37**

M
Meanders of the Cuckmere **52**
Milton Gate in 1937 **75**

O
Osprey Platform **58**

S
Seven Sisters **4, 5, 17**

W
Westdean Rectory **12**
Wilmington Lake **57, 79, 83**

ABOUT THE AUTHOR

Patrick Coulcher was educated at Eastbourne College and from an early age became interested in natural history and the countryside. He graduated from the Royal Air Force College, Cranwell in 1957 and spent the next 38 years as a Fighter Pilot and Instructor on many different types of aircraft. When he retired in 1992 he became actively involved in issues concerning the environment and conservation. He gives illustrated talks on these subjects to numerous groups and has published several books on natural history.

The author on Folkington Downs

Osprey